THE WEEKLY AHA!

The Weekly Aha!

---

52 Inspirations for Innovation, Peak Performance & Team Success

ARASH ARABI

Sprint Agile

Disclaimer

"If you want to build a ship, don't drum up people to collect wood and don't assign them tasks and work, but rather teach them to long for the endless immensity of the sea."

~ Antoine de Saint-Exupery

CONTENTS

PREFACE

Welcome to a journey of transformation, where each week unfolds a new chapter of growth and excellence for you and your team. This book is not a collection of random ideas; it's a guiding light for change, a catalyst for innovation, and a blueprint for building high-performing teams.

Every leader aspires to lead teams that are innovative, proactive, and consistently deliver exceptional results. However, the reality often falls short of this ideal. It's a significant challenge to foster an environment that promotes growth, capability development, and innovation, especially when teams are under constant delivery pressure, every task is a high priority, and project deadlines loom large. Traditional Organisational Learning and Development programs often don't meet the mark in these scenarios. Online programs lack engagement, and full-day classroom training is typically impractical for teams juggling high-priority tasks.

This was one of the main challenges I faced in my career as an engineering manager and later as an enterprise coach. The question was, how do you assist leaders in large organisations to create an environment where teams become innovative and high-performing without compromising on delivery? And to add to the complexity, how do you achieve this at scale?

My solution was a microlearning program delivered over several weeks. Every Monday, I would send out an email to the team with a thought-provoking inspiration. These emails aimed to teach the reader something new, tell a story, provide practical tips, or introduce a new concept.

However, these weekly inspirations needed to be more than just nuggets of information. They needed to spark conversations and create a ripple effect. I wanted these inspirations to be the topic of discussion during lunch breaks and to keep resurfacing in conversations throughout the week. To achieve this, these emails had to inspire a sense of awe and wonder in the reader.

This initiative became one of my most effective strategies as an enterprise coach. It helped to upskill entire divisions at scale, creating a ripple effect of positive change throughout the organisation. It sparked dialogues and broadened horizons—all sustained over extended periods.

Now, this book brings together the 52 most impactful inspirations from that journey. Aligned with the 52 weeks of the year, it provides a wealth of educational content for you and your team. Each piece is crafted to be absorbed quickly yet linger long in the mind, encouraging immediate action and ongoing change. The ultimate aim is to cultivate high-performing teams and organisations, inspiring team members and leaders alike to refine their approach to work.

These inspirations are more than words; they are the seeds of wonder and awe. They are the sparks that ignite the human spirit to strive for change. When shared consistently, they have the power to reshape mindsets, alter behaviours, and elevate performance, transforming the ordinary into the extraordinary.

Each inspiration presented here carries enough weight to be the subject of its own book. Unlike many business books that stretch a single idea over hundreds of pages, this book respects your intelligence and time, condensing a wealth of content into concise and impactful messages. By reading this book, you are essentially reading 52 distinct books. We're all quick learners, so there's no need for endless repetition. As eloquently put by William Shakespeare, 'brevity is the soul of wit.'

I encourage you to continue this tradition and share these inspirations with your team or organisation. This book provides you with a year's worth of content for weekly emails. When you do share, please include a reference to this book and a link to my website for those interested in delving deeper—a URL can be found on the back cover.

There's no prescribed order to read this book; feel free to dive in at any point. However, if you share these inspirations weekly, following the sequence can guide your readers on a structured learning journey.

And for science fiction enthusiasts, keep an eye out for easter eggs hidden within the text, particularly in the titles of the inspirations. Enjoy the discoveries as you embark on this adventure.

Inspiration 1: How to Work Smarter, Not Harder!

The first topic in this series is arguably the most important one: the concept of "working smarter" and the allegory of "sharpening the axe".

Imagine you're a lumberjack paid per tree. To earn enough to pay for your bills and support your family, you need to chop down ten trees each day. On the first day, you have no trouble cutting ten trees. However, after a few days, you find it increasingly difficult to cut down trees, and you have to work harder.

One day, despite your hard work, you realise you've only managed to cut down nine trees. As time passes, the task becomes even more challenging, and after a few days, you can only fell eight trees.

An experienced lumberjack notices your struggle and suggests that you sharpen your axe, as it's becoming dull. But you refuse, saying you don't have the time. You've already used all your savings, maxed out your credit card, and you feel you must spend all your time cutting as many trees as possible to make ends meet.

But this is not smart, the longer you neglect to sharpen your axe, the fewer trees you'll be able to cut, and the more time you'll need to restore your axe's sharpness. If you sharpen your axe today, it might only take 10 minutes, but if you wait, it could take half an hour. You feel you are trapped in a rat race.

But no one is going to hand you a new axe. Your only option is to take a break, bite the bullet, and sharpen your axe.

This week, I invite you to consider how you can work smarter. What steps can you take now to increase your efficiency in the future? How can you "sharpen your axe"?

"Give me six hours to chop down a tree and I will spend the first four sharpening the axe." - Abraham Lincoln:

| 2 |

Inspiration 2: The Wright Way to Fly!

About 120 years ago, the Wright brothers achieved the first controlled flight with a powered, heavier-than-air aircraft. However, the Wright brothers were not the only team in this race to flight. The most promising group was led by a well-respected and accomplished scientist, Samuel Langley.

Langley had secured significant government funding and had a team of engineers working on his flying machine called "The Great Aerodrome". However, as you all know, Langley is not known for achieving flight. Langley's Aerodrome crashed immediately on takeoff in front of many reporters and a large crowd.

While Langley's team were meticulously solving technical problems and perfecting The Great Aerodrome, the Wright brothers were experimenting with cheap prototypes they made in their bicycle shop. And a short while after Langley's crash, the

Wright brothers achieved flight during one of their many test attempts.

What Langley could not achieve with all his experience, his engineers, and $50,000 of funding, the Wright brothers achieved with less than $1,000 and the right approach to prototyping and experimentation.

This week, I invite you to think about how you can have a more experimental approach to problem-solving. How can you prototype quickly and then polish those prototypes instead of trying to come up with a perfect solution in the first attempt?

"If we all worked on the assumption that what is accepted as true is really true, there would be little hope of advance."
~Orville Wright

| 3 |

Inspiration 3: Messi's Winning Mindset!

Lionel Messi is one of the best Soccer players in the world. He plays in the forward position and currently captains both Inter Miami Football Club and the Argentina national team. As a forward, his role in the game is to be a striker. Basically, he is responsible for scoring goals. That is his job description.

However, there are many well-known instances where Messi has saved his team by moving into a fullback position and blocking the opposing team's striker from scoring a goal. Messi's role is not a fullback; it is not in his job description to defend. Yet, when he sees an opportunity, he jumps in and does all he can to save their team.

Similarly, in our teams, we want to move away from the mindset of "doing my job" to the mindset of "getting the job done".

Doing my job ➡ Getting the job done

One of the key skills that helps us move towards the "getting the job done" mentality is resourcefulness. Resourcefulness is the ability to find quick and clever ways to overcome difficulties. A resourceful person thinks outside the box when faced with roadblocks, and instead of giving up, he/she does whatever it takes to get the job done.

Resourceful people are creative, persistent, and open-minded. They persevere towards the end goal but easily and quickly change tactics when blocked. One of the greatest assets of resourceful people is their large network and personal relationships.

When resourcefulness is paired up with a teamwork spirit, we become an unstoppable force. We will do whatever it takes to help our team reach its goals. At the end of the day, we must remember that we are playing a team sport; either we all win together, or we lose together.

| 4 |

Inspiration 4: Talk Your Way into New Thinking!

This inspiration is about the power of words. It is accepted that the way we think influences the way we talk. But also, the reverse is true. Our choice of words when talking influences how we think and our mindsets.

In his book "Turn the Ship Around", David Marquet talks about using empowering phrases rather than disempowering phrases so that we think and act more empowered.

'The key to your team becoming more proactive rests in the language subordinates and superiors use. Here is a short list of "disempowered phrases" that passive followers use: Request permission to . . . I would like to . . . What should I do about . . . . Do you think we should . . . Could we . . . Here is a short list of "empowered phrases" that active doers use: I intend to . . . I plan on . . . I will . . . We will . . .' — L. David Marquet, Turn the Ship Around!: A True Story of Turning Followers into Leaders

✗	✓
I would like to . . .	I intend to . . .
What should I do about . . .	I plan on . . .
Do you think we should . . .	I will . . .
Could we . . .	We will . . .
← "disempowered phrases"	"empowered phrases" →

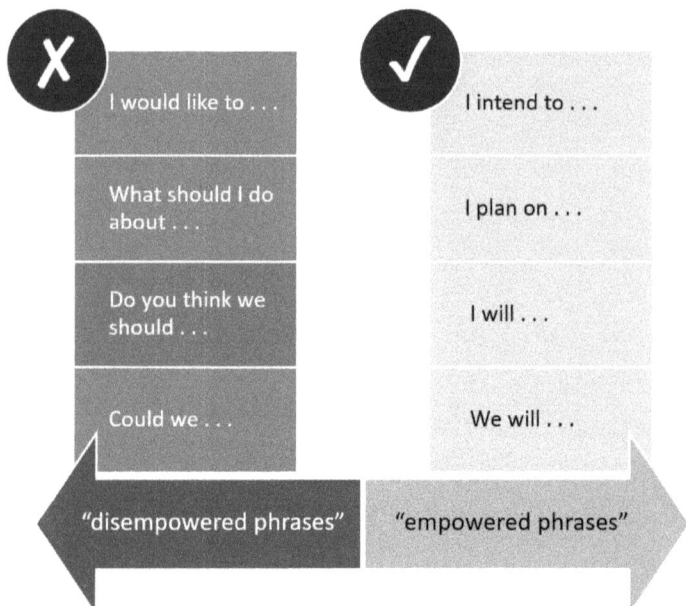

Words define how we think, and how we think defines how we act. By using empowering phrases rather than disempowering ones, we will rewire our brains to think and behave differently.

The human mind works in intriguing ways. We normally assume that our mindset and beliefs determine our actions, but the reverse is also true. Our actions, in fact, have a profound influence on shaping our mindset and beliefs.

For example, if we smile for no reason, we automatically become a happier person in that moment.[1] Similarly, if we use empowering words and phrases, we start to become more confident and empowered.

| 5 |

Inspiration 5: Crafting Creativity, Stitching Innovation!

Innovation happens through exploration and discovery. To explore and discover, we need to slow down and reflect. We must dedicate and protect solid blocks of time to step out of the delivery mindset, reflect together, and strategise collaboratively.

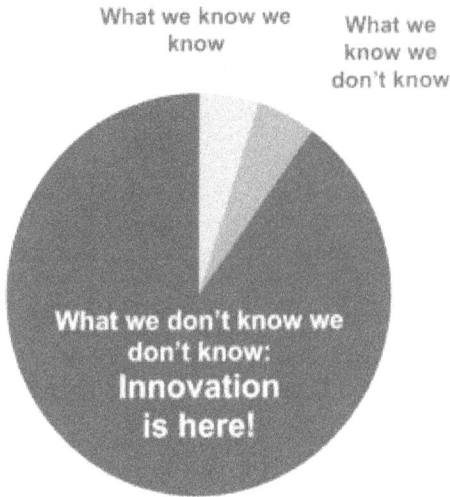

What we know we know

What we know we don't know

What we don't know we don't know: Innovation is here!

In one of his lectures, the renowned American Systems Scientist Dr Peter Senge[2] shared a story about a program at Hewlett-Packard (HP) aimed at identifying networks of people within the organisation and how they contributed to product innovation. Surprisingly, they discovered that approximately a quarter to a third of their most significant product innovation ideas originated from a single network of about 35 women in a specific office. This was quite a surprise for the managers, given the disproportionate impact of this small group of women within an organisation comprising tens of thousands of people distributed globally.

Upon further investigation, they found that these individuals were all the women in the quilting circle. This perplexed the managers, so they brought in these individuals for interviews to understand what made them so effective at innovating. They found that the dedicated time the quilting circle members spent together regularly —socialising and talking about various topics in an unstructured way—created a unique opportunity for reflection and exploration, resulting in those individuals contributing significantly to the organisation.

Another example of how social interactions can foster innovation is seen in the approach taken by the CEO of Bose. He made a rule that no one could have coffee at their desks. If you wanted coffee, you had to go to the kitchen. This made sure people had to slow down, chat with each other, and share ideas while having a cup of coffee. This simple act created a space for people to be more creative.

To be innovative, we need to dedicate regular time and space to get together in-person, just for the sake of getting together, having a good time, socialising, and enjoying spending time together.

So, I invite you today to think about how you can create a venue like this. A venue without any agendas and without any specific problems to solve. A venue where people can meet up regularly, do something they enjoy, and get to know each other better. You never know, this could be where the next big idea comes from.

| 6 |

Inspiration 6: When the Amygdala Hijacks Your Brain!

There is a primitive part of our brains deep in the limbic system called the amygdala. One of the key responsibilities of amygdala is the fight-or-flight response and regulating some of our primitive emotions, such as fear and pleasure. There is another part of the brain called the prefrontal cortex. It covers the front of our neocortex and is considered the "executive centre" of the brain. Think of it as your brain's CEO.

Sometimes, when we feel strong emotions, the amygdala overreacts, takes over the prefrontal cortex, and disrupts our ability to guide our behaviour effectively. This event is called an "amygdala hijack".

Prefrontal cortex:
Executive center of the brain, the CEO.

Amygdala:
Primitive part of brain triggering flight or fight response in response to threat or some emotions.

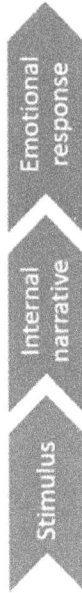

Stimulus → Internal narrative → Emotional response

Amygdala hijack :
Amygdala overreacts and takes over prefrontal cortex and disrupt our abilities to guide our behavior effectively.

With practice, Amygdala hijack can be reversed using techniques such as perspective taking and mindfulness

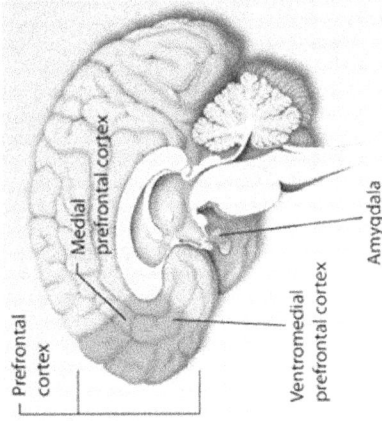

Amygdala hijack typically results in impulsive behaviours and is usually followed by an emotional hangover. Once the

strong emotions wear off, we often feel guilty. Now, imagine if you could stay in full control during such events. Imagine if you could remain calm in moments of stress and use your cognitive smarts to come up with a clever and clean solution or response for whatever you faced.

Well, the good news is that you can, and it's not that difficult. You just need to practise, like learning any skill. The same neural connections that allow the amygdala to hijack your prefrontal cortex also allow the prefrontal cortex to keep the amygdala in check.[3]

Some mindfulness techniques that help reverse amygdala hijack include:

- Taking three slow and deep breaths.
- Slowly taping your finger on your body (one tap every 3 – 4 seconds).
- Touching something and focusing on its texture.

Different people may find different techniques more effective. For example, I find that focusing on surface texture works best in calming me down when I feel strong emotions.

| 7 |

Inspiration 7: What Is 'Agile', and Where Did It Come From?

Which one is more agile: a car, a kangaroo, or a bullet train?

Of course, the answer is a kangaroo, despite not being the fastest. Contrary to what many organisations believe, agility is not *necessarily* about speed or rapid delivery. It's about our ability to respond to changing conditions quickly and easily. Also, we have to remember that agility is not binary; rather, it's a spectrum. For example, a kangaroo is more agile than a car, which in turn is more agile than a bullet train.[4]

More Agile   Less Agile

We cannot say this organisation is agile and this one is not. Instead, we could say this organisation is more agile than the other one.

Now, where did the buzzword "Agile" originate, and how did it find its way into organisations?

In February 2001, 17 visionary thought leaders in the software delivery industry convened in a ski lodge in Utah. These individuals were independently revolutionising the ways of working at their companies and achieving exceptional results. There were a lot of similarities in their methods. So, they decided to collaborate and attempt to summarise the essence of their work in a single manifesto.

They gathered at the Snowbird Ski Resort from the 12th to the 14th of February 2001. They had a lot of fun: they skied, had drinks, did a little bit of work in between, and formulated the "Agile Manifesto".

Since then, the "Agile" movement has evolved far beyond just software development. We now talk about Agile Product Development and Business Agility. The word 'agile' is now used in its proper dictionary meaning: to be nimble and respond to changing conditions easily and quickly. Today, instead of *doing* "Agile" with a capital "A" as a method or process, we aim to *be* 'agile' with a lowercase 'a', as in being nimble and responding to change quickly.

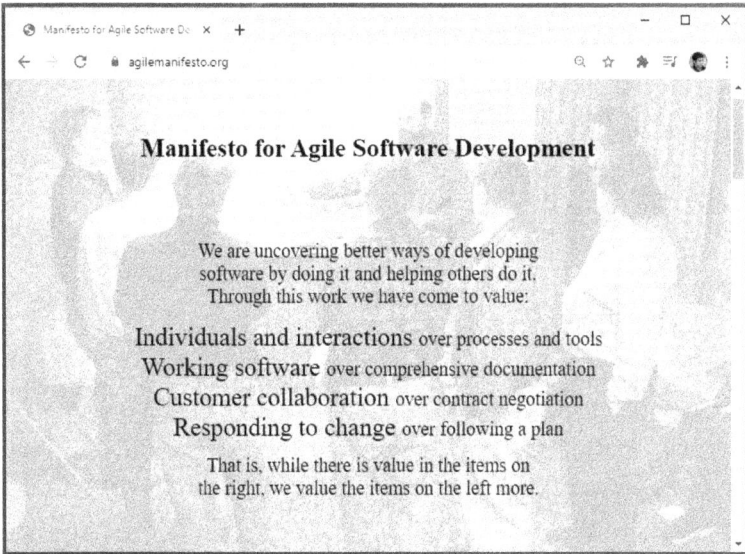

The Image above illustrates the four values of the Agile Manifesto.

Note that the manifesto states: "That is, while there is value in the items on the right, we value the items on the left more." This is the most important statement in the manifesto. It's all about balance.

To learn more about the Agile Manifesto, its four values, and twelve principles, please visit agilemanifesto.org.

| 8 |

Inspiration 8: Painting Features Prints Dollars!

One of the key concepts of Agile is the idea of incremental value delivery. But what does it actually mean to deliver incrementally? The best metaphor to explain incremental delivery is painting vs printing.

Non-incremental value delivery

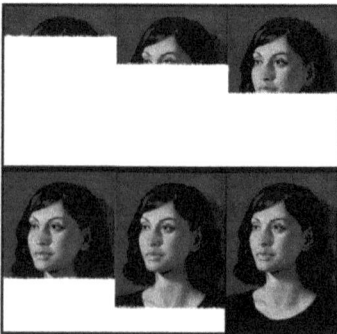

Incremental value delivery

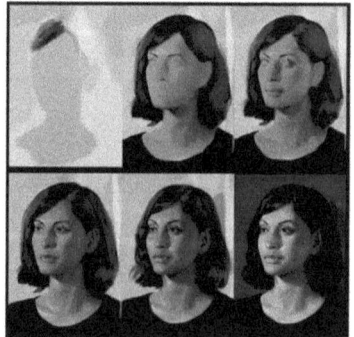

To illustrate this, I'd like to share a personal experience. A few years ago, when the product "Grammarly" first entered the market, I saw their ad and thought, "This seems like a useful product. I should purchase it." It was close to the end of the financial year, so I thought I could also claim the expense on my tax return. I went ahead and purchased a Grammarly subscription. But to my surprise, I didn't receive a tax invoice! I looked up their FAQ on their website and found an entry that stated, "We have not yet developed the tax invoice feature. If you need a tax invoice, please email us, and we will send you your invoice." Naturally, I sent them an email and received my invoice.

In this scenario, Grammarly made a tactical decision to release their product to the market even though it was not "complete" and had missing features. This does not mean the product was low quality. The features that were released were of high quality and functioned well. It simply did not have all the features that you might expect from such a product.

Had Grammarly waited to launch until the tax invoice feature was ready, I wouldn't have been able to use the product when I needed it. This would have also delayed their revenue generation. More importantly, if this delay pushed the release past the end of the financial year, they would have missed out on a substantial market segment. These are customers who buy such products to decrease their taxes.

When we develop any type of product, we should think strategically. How can we slice for value so that we deliver a subset of features to a high standard of quality, and then incrementally add more features?

So, this week, I invite you to reflect: "Are you delivering value to your stakeholders simply iteratively, or are you also delivering value incrementally?"

| 9 |

Inspiration 9: Who's the Boss? Everyone!

How do you create an environment where teams can be fully autonomous, proactive, creative, and innovative? According to David Marquet, the answer is by moving the authority to where the information is[5].

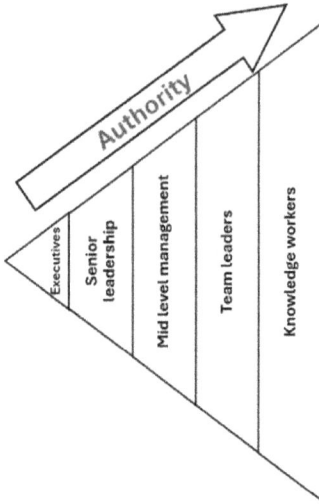

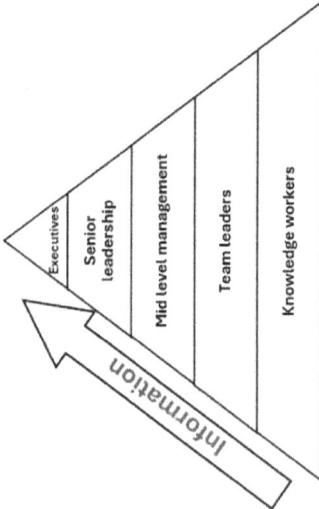

"Don't move information to authority, move authority to the information." ~ David Marquet

But you may be concerned that if we give teams authority and control, they may make mistakes, which could result in adverse outcomes for the company! Yes, that's true, but we can significantly reduce this risk and prevent things from going wrong.

The formula for this model's success rests on two pillars: *competence* and *clarity*. Team members need to be competent and clear on their objectives in order to make good decisions – decisions as good, if not better, than those the leader would make.

That transition process starts by pushing the team slightly beyond its comfort zone. Team competence and clarity are then built within these boundaries. As a team's competence and clarity increase each day, its level of control should go up. It's essential to give the team a bit more control than its level of competence and clarity to accelerate its learning and growth.

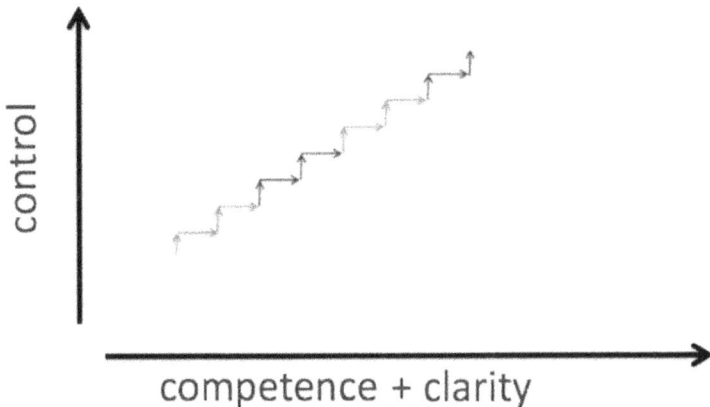

A great leader keeps the team in their learning zone. As the team learns and builds competence and clarity, their learning zone becomes their comfort zone. Then, the leader must give more control to move the team to a new learning zone. If too much control is given without a corresponding rise in competence and clarity, the team may end up in the panic zone, likely resulting in things going wrong. By constantly expanding a team's learning zone, a great leader will, over time, empower it to become fully in control and independent.

A leader can accelerate the process above by asking coaching questions. For example, when the team members are given authority to make decisions on something beyond their level of competence and clarity, a leader can ask them, "What does success look like to you?"

| 10 |

Inspiration 10: Scrum: Where Coders Become Rugby Stars!

Scrum is the most popular Agile Framework. Nearly every software development team in the world uses some Scrum framework elements. Since its inception in the 1990s, Scrum has evolved beyond a framework only for software delivery. Today, many product development and operational teams across various organisations use Scrum to deliver value more effectively.

The Scrum framework is based on small, cross-functional, self-managing teams that have the capability to deliver a slice of value within a short iteration of time (typically two weeks).

The term "Scrum" originates from rugby. But why is it called Scrum? Scrum was developed in the early 1990s by Ken Schwaber and Jeff Sutherland, who drew inspiration from an article in the Harvard Business Review.

In 1986, two Japanese management professors, Takeuchi and Nonaka, published a paper titled "The new new product development game" at the Harvard Business Review. In this paper, the authors used rugby scrum as a metaphor as opposed to relay racing. They argued that traditional "*Waterfall* development" with its phase gates and approvals is like a relay race where one person passes the baton to the next person and so on.

They argued instead of that we should have a scrum-like approach to product development. Scrum is like a huddle where the team collectively inch towards the goal. From the outside, it may look a bit messy and unclear. We don't know who has the ball, who is doing what, and who is pushing where, but from the inside, every single subtle movement is calculated with skill and precision. Every single player knows exactly what they should do, and the team works together without anyone telling them what to do.

Similarly, a product development team needs to collaborate closely. They need to have skill and precision, and they need to know where they are going and how to work with each other to move towards their goal. The managers from the outside need to get comfortable with not having full control and trusting the team to do the right thing. Unlike *Waterfall*, Scrum has no sign-offs, phase gates, or approvals.

However, transparency is one of the pillars of Scrum. Both the team and management must do everything they can to radiate information and make things as transparent as possible.

If you are interested in learning more about Scrum, Please listen to the comprehensive podcast I did with NRG to perform titled "Defeat the Enemy Within".[6]

ACTIVE CEO PODCAST #151 ARASH ARABI DEFEAT THE ENEMY WITHIN

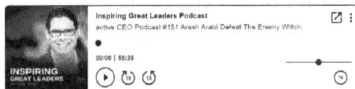

| 11 |

Inspiration 11: The Jedi, the Timelord, and the Outlaws of the Galaxy!

Scrum, the most widely used Agile framework, defines three specific roles for the team (Scrum Master, Product Owner, and Developer).

The Scrum master is responsible for facilitating the execution, removing impediments, and providing servant leadership. The product owner is responsible for defining and prioritising the product backlog. And developers are responsible for developing the product. It's important to note that "developer" here does not refer solely to computer programmers but to anyone on the team who contributes to the product's creation (essentially everyone except the Scrum Master and the Product Owner).

I have written a fun poem comparing the Scrum roles with science fiction characters. This is an entertaining metaphor for understanding the roles, please don't take it too seriously!

The Scrum Master is like Obi-Wan Kenobi

The Scrum Master is the glue for the team.

He has excellent relationships with everyone.

He is a facilitator.

Makes sure the processes that the team agree upon are followed.

He is the impediment bulldozer.

He uses a lightsabre to open the path for storm developers (stormtroopers) to move forward into enemy territory.

He is diplomatic but not political, witty and clever but righteous.

He travels across the galaxy to facilitate and remove impediments.

And most importantly, he uses "The Force" to sense impediments before they even emerge.

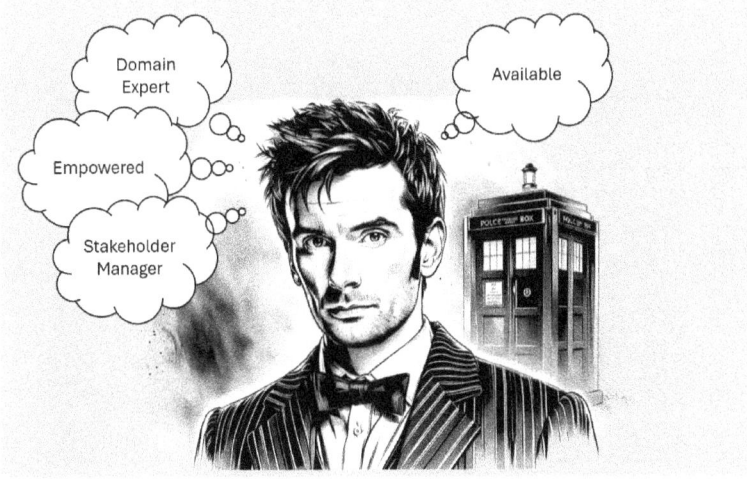

The Product Owner is like The Doctor

He has the weight of the world on his shoulders.

He prioritises. Some lives need to be sacrificed to save the universe. And the product owner needs to live with those decisions for the rest of his life.

There is so much on his mind, so many responsibilities, so many balls to juggle, but so little time. Needs a TARDIS to go back in time to finish those Jira tickets just in time.

He has made so many mistakes, but at the end of the day, he has saved the product and the universe so many times.

He is the best negotiator in the world. Can negotiate Daleks and Iron Men out of blowing up the planet.

He knows almost everything. He has breadth of knowledge.

He finds information and provides it in a consumable format.

He is always available any time anywhere. He has a TARDIS.

And most importantly he is empowered to make decisions.

The Developers are like the Guardians of the Galaxy

They are NOT superheroes. They don't have superpowers. Except for maybe Groot.

They have T-shaped skills. Highly skilled at one thing but also a little skilled at a few other things.

They are resourceful.

They may have their differences, but they collaborate really well.

They come up with ingenious plans, and then improvise when things don't go according to the plan.

They cover for each other.

They may look a bit harsh at first, but actually they are prepared to die for each other.

They all have their quirks, but do the right thing at the end of the day.

And most importantly they do whatever it takes, *whatever it takes*, to get the job done.

| 12 |

Inspiration 12: Quadruple Quick!

Imagine you are moving house and would like a new internet connection installed at your new property. That can't possibly be a pleasant experience! You call your Internet service provider, and they ask when you would like the technician to come down and install your service. That's a bit of a surprise, but you tell them I would like my service installed on September 17th between 8:00 and 8:30 am. Then, to your surprise, on September 17th, precisely at 8:00 am, the technician comes down and installs your service and leaves before 8:30 am.

What do you think? Is this even possible? How amazing would it be to get such service quality from our network providers? From the customer's point of view, we don't care about the complexities and challenges that an organisation has to face internally behind the scenes; all we care about is receiving high-quality products and services efficiently and effectively. To illustrate how providing exceptional quality to our customers is possible, we must first understand how efficiency works.

There are two types of efficiencies: flow efficiency and resource efficiency (resource utilisation). Flow efficiency is efficiency from the customer's perspective, while resource efficiency is efficiency from the perspective of the person doing the work.

Niklas Modig, the author of "This is Lean: Resolving the Efficiency Paradox", tells us the story of how the Swedish healthcare system revolutionised its process for diagnosing ADHD patients. Patients had to go through a multi-step process of seeing multiple doctors and clinics, often having to wait long between appointments. Modig uses the analogy of what type of movie it would be if we put a camera on the doctors' shoulders vs. the patients' shoulders.

If we put a video camera on the shoulders of the doctors, we see they are working hard all the time (it is going to be an action movie), but if we put a video camera on the shoulders of the patients, it is not going to be much of an action movie. There will be weeks of waiting and a few hours of doctor consultation in between.

This is because we have increased the utilisation efficiency at the expense of flow efficiency. It's an economic principle that, past a certain point, increasing resource utilisation will not result in an increase in flow.

What does a 100% utilised highway look like?

What does a 95% utilised memory, CPU, or hard disk look like?

So, how can we prioritise flow efficiency over resource efficiency? The answer is to re-organise our system and ways of working to maximise flow efficiency first and then resource efficiency.

Take, for instance, how the Swedish healthcare system revolutionised the ADHD diagnosis process timeline through a strategic redesign. They created a cross-functional team that brought together all the experts needed to diagnose ADHD. Rather than the patients having to go through multiple assessments by different specialists in different clinics, in the new process, the patients would go through a single assessment by a group of specialists working as a team.

Instead of each doctor working separately with their own list of patients, they created a unified team of specialists who worked together. They used a single board to visualise the workflow and track the progress of each patient through the diagnosis process. They even used patient headshots on the board to add a personal touch.

By doing this, the ADHD diagnosis process was reduced from 4 months to 3 weeks. That is over 4x improvement in delivery speed.[7]

So, I ask you today, what can you do to quadruple your delivery speed? Here's a hint - look for steps in the delivery process or value stream where work is performed by different silos. Remember, each handover inherently causes queues and delays, and also introduces the risk of miscommunication or errors.

| 13 |

Inspiration 13: Upside-Down Management: Inverting the Iron Triangle!

Traditional project management theory defines three parameters constraining product quality in a project. These constraints are time, cost, and scope (requirements). A traditional project manager would balance and trade off these parameters to manage the delivery of the project.

This concept is also known as the 'Iron Triangle' or 'Triple Constraints'. The idea is that if we want to change one of these constraints, we must adjust the other two accordingly to prevent a decline in quality. To illustrate how this works, let's do a thought experiment. Let's suppose you want to build a wall, and you have hired a bricklayer to build the wall for you. The bricklayer comes and looks at the site, does some measurements, and says, 'This wall needs X number of bricks, and it will take me Y number of minutes to lay each brick, so it will take me two full days to build the wall. So, assuming I start working right now, I can give you a finished wall by the end of the day tomorrow.'

Then you tell the bricklayer, 'I need you to finish this wall by the end of the day today.' But the bricklayer's response is, 'Well, I can give you half a wall by the end of the day today.' You point out that it's not possible as the painter is coming tomorrow to paint the whole wall. The bricklayer says, 'OK, I can build the whole wall for you today, but I need to hire a helping hand. The two of us working together means we should be able to finish the wall in a day instead of two days. But it will cost you a lot more because these contractors have higher day rates, and it's also short notice.' You respond, 'No, I want you to finish the wall in one day only by yourself. I can't afford to pay for the extra contractor.' The poor bricklayer has no choice as he needs the job, so he agrees to build the whole wall in one day without any help. Inevitably, he will build a low-quality wall. As he rushes through the job, the bricks will not be aligned well, and the cement will not be applied according to safety standards.

This metaphor is for understanding the iron triangle, and of course, software development projects are a lot more complex than this simplified example. To make managing these constraints easier, Agile project management attempts to invert the iron triangle. In traditional Waterfall project management, typically, the scope is fixed, and time and cost are derived, but in Agile, we want to fix the time and cost and derive the scope.

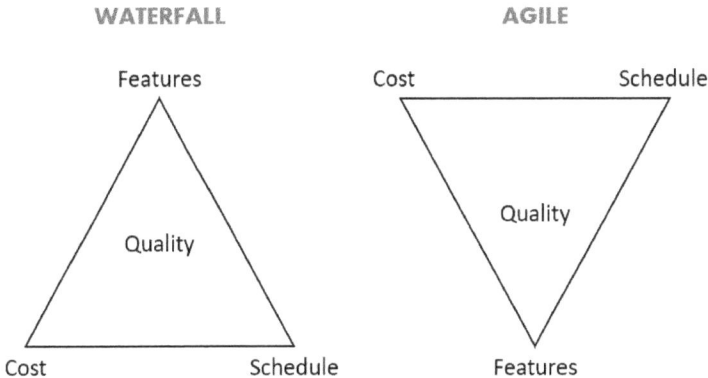

WATERFALL

AGILE

Features

Cost   Schedule

Quality

Quality

Cost   Schedule

Features

Now, let's further unpack how this works. In Waterfall project management, more or less, what we do aligns with the following steps:

Problem	• We have a problem to solve
Solution	• A number of experts and analysts get together & hypothesise a solution to the problem
Specs	• They define the scope and requirements specification for the solution
WBS	• A Work Breakdown Structure for the solution is created
Planning	• Tasks in the WBS are estimated, dependencies are identified & a Gantt chart is created
Time estimate	• Based on the critical path project timelines are estimated
Cost estimate	• Based on the skills and number of resources needed for tasks, cost is estimated
Implement-ation	• Then we start building the project

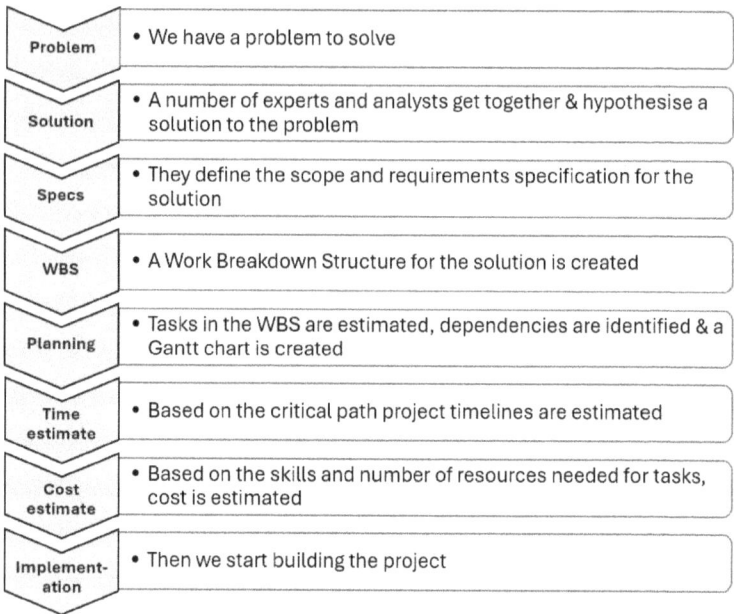

For example, let's say the problem we are trying to solve is reducing the number of calls to the call centre by 50%. We hypothesise that if we build a chatbot, this will reduce the number of calls to the call centre by 50%. We will go ahead and define the requirements for the chatbot. Then, based on those requirements, we identify what skills we need; for example, we may need X number of Java developers and Y number of platform engineers. Then, we estimate the tasks and user stories that those engineers need to deliver. Based on how many people, how many days, and the salary of those engineers, we derive the cost and timeline of the project. We put a project team together and then deliver the chatbot according to the plan we came up with.

In Agile, we want to invert the iron triangle, so we do the exact opposite of the above.

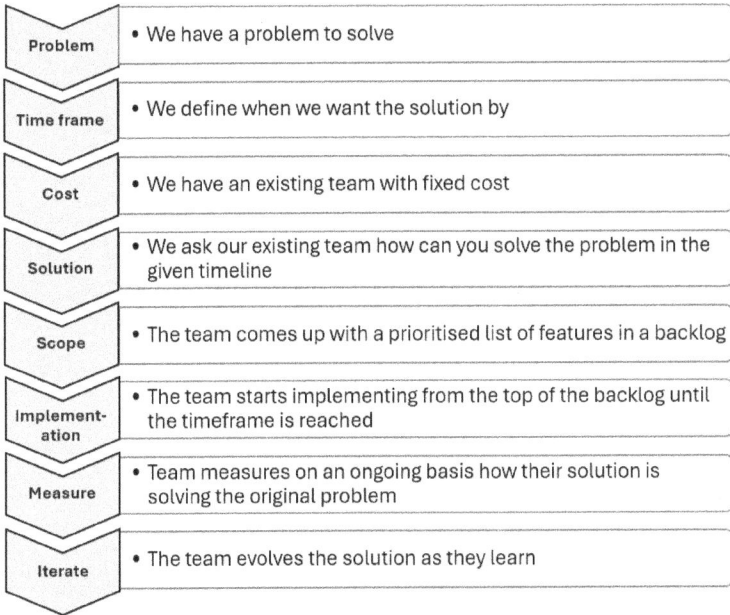

Problem	• We have a problem to solve
Time frame	• We define when we want the solution by
Cost	• We have an existing team with fixed cost
Solution	• We ask our existing team how can you solve the problem in the given timeline
Scope	• The team comes up with a prioritised list of features in a backlog
Implement-ation	• The team starts implementing from the top of the backlog until the timeframe is reached
Measure	• Team measures on an ongoing basis how their solution is solving the original problem
Iterate	• The team evolves the solution as they learn

Now, let's say we want to solve the same problem using an Agile approach. We want to reduce the number of calls to the call centre by 50%. We take this business problem to our existing team. The existing team asks us when we want the solution delivered. Let's say, for example, we want the solution in six months. Let's suppose the team costs $100,000 to run per month. So, we will know immediately that the cost of the project will be $600k. Then, the team goes away and, based on their existing skills, capabilities, and knowledge, comes up with a solution that can be delivered within six months and will reduce the number of calls to the call centre by 50%. But they may come up with a drastically different solution than what we had in mind! Maybe instead of a chatbot, they decide we should build an FAQ page.

Also, it's important to note that scope/requirements are flexible in this approach, and the team will come up with a prioritised backlog of features. They will go through as many features as possible within the six-month time frame, and based on what they learn, they may or may not pivot the solution and change the upcoming features in the backlog. The team will release features regularly and measure their work's impact on the original business hypothesis. For example, they will measure on an ongoing basis how much their work has reduced the number of calls to the call centre.

The beauty of this approach is that it enables us to focus on what really matters. That is, achieving the ultimate business outcome rather than just pumping out features and sticking to unvalidated hypotheses about the benefits of those features.

| 14 |

Inspiration 14: Making Work Flow!

You may have heard the word Kanban before. Kanban means "signboard" in Japanese and usually refers to the board that agile teams use to visualise and track their work.

But Kanban can also refer to the Kanban Method, a management approach developed by David J. Anderson and inspired by the Toyota Production System.

A simplistic view of the Kanban method might suggest it's just Scrum without the iterations. However, this is far from the truth. Kanban provides a set of principles, practices, and techniques that can help you improve service delivery, regardless of your team's function.

If you want to improve your team's performance, one of the things you can do is to start experimenting with Kanban principles. The diagram below illustrates the six Kanban principles and provides some examples of how to implement them within your team.[8]

Visualise the work	• Just cards on the wall is not enough. • Visualise work classes, people, states, delays, blockages, and everything you need.
Limit your WIP	• Are you limiting Work in progress? Do you have hard WIP limits on your board columns? • Limiting WIP, increases throughput, even if staff feel less productive.
Manage flow	• Do you have different swim-lanes for expedite, normal, & improvement work? • Have you separated each workflow state into "doing" and "ready for"?
Implement feedback loops	• Do you have the right meetings, ceremonies, & artefacts to close feedback loops? • Do you have meetings to review strategy, risk, delivery, & planning with stakeholders?
Create explicit policies	• Are your team's policies & processes explicitly defined, documented, & visualised? • Kanban process needs to be mechanical, but team needs to improve the process on regular basis. Don't forget: Individuals and interactions over processes & tools.
Continuous collaborative evolutionary improvement	• Are you devising experiments on regular basis to improve and measure? • Do you have dedicated capacity and a swim-lane on your board for sharpening the axe?

Below are three easy takeaways that most teams can focus on to improve their performance.

- Dedicate capacity for improvement work and visualise it on the board. Ensure that actions from your retrospectives (reflection meetings) are visualised on the same board as your regular user stories (delivery work).
- For every board column, have a "ready for" and "doing" sub-columns.
- Jira and other virtual boards are not as effective as physical boards. Consider what essential aspects are not visualised on your Jira board and create a dashboard to display all necessary information.

| 15 |

Inspiration 15: The Lean, Mean, Improvement Machine!

When you make an improvement in your team, such as process improvement, automation, efficiency enhancement, adoption of agile practices, or any other form of improvement, you often end up with additional time and capacity. This extra time can be used in various ways, such as:

- Taking on more work.
- Investing in further innovation and improvement.
- Helping other teams with their workload.
- Helping other teams improve.
- Celebrating or doing team building activities.
- Resting!
- And more ...

What do you think is the best use of the extra time you gain from improvements?

Before answering this question, I'd like to introduce the concept of value stream maps. Below is an example of a value stream map when you order a burger at a fast-food joint:

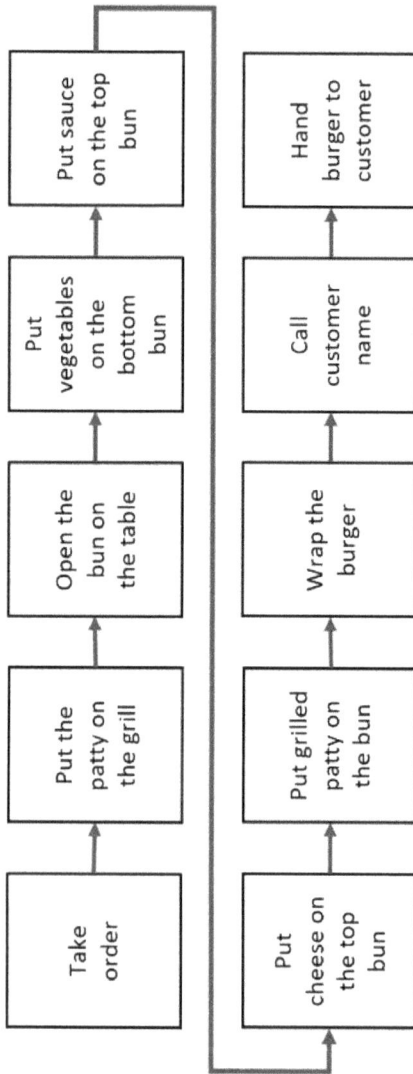

Of course, other activities happen before this value stream begins, such as entering the shop, checking the menu, deciding what you'll have, and queuing at the register. Similarly, there are activities that happen after receiving your burger, like eating it, digesting it, and so on.

Similarly, you can map the value stream of delivering new initiatives in organisations as shown in the diagram below:

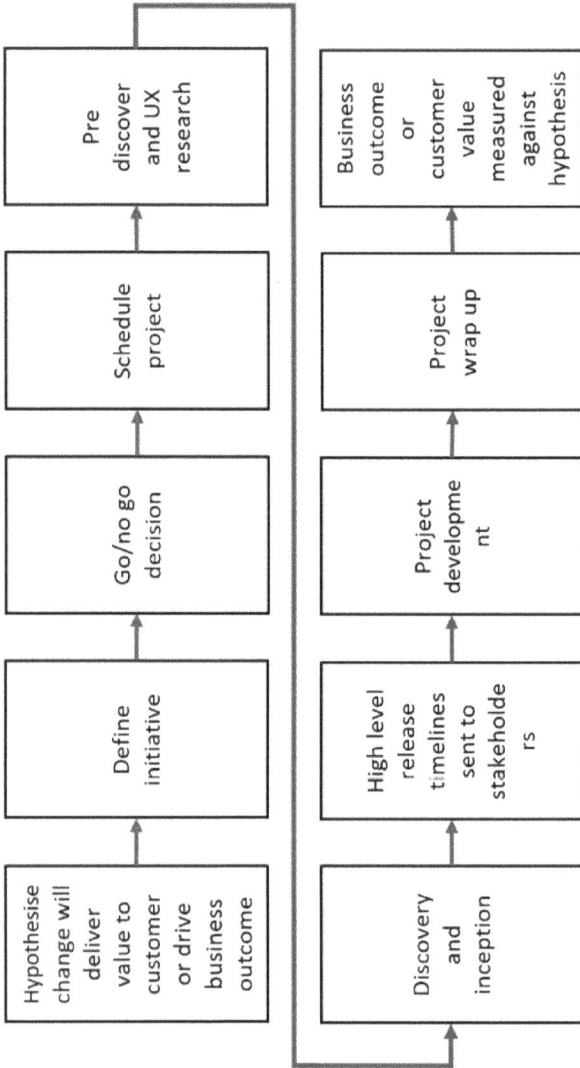

Just like the burger example, there are activities that happen before the value stream starts and after it ends. When mapping a value stream, you need to decide on the boundaries of your value stream. What will you consider as your starting point, and what will you consider the point where value is delivered?

Now, let's imagine in the burger value stream, the person who is responsible for putting vegetables on the bun suddenly finds a more efficient way of doing their job and can work twice as fast. What would the implications of this be?

This likely results in the entire system slowing down! Because, as this person is working faster, they will be creating an inventory queue for the next step of the process. Also, the time it takes to grill the patty remains unchanged.

The burger value stream is a simple and straightforward process. When we do product development, our processes are much more complex. We have feedback loops between the steps, many sub-activities, and numerous stakeholders involved in those sub-activities.

So, if you make an improvement in your team, it will be challenging to know if taking on more work will enhance the entire end-to-end delivery, resulting in better outcomes for the organisation, or if it will cause more problems elsewhere in the value stream.

In technical terms, optimising a part of a system will likely result in a sub-optimal whole. This brings us back to our initial question: what should you do with the extra time you gain from improvement activities?

"After you make an improvement, the last thing you should do is more work."

-Prager's Law

We know that the last thing you want to do after making an improvement is taking on more work. Dan Prager, the creator of the Prager's Law, suggests perhaps you should first celebrate and then invest that time in more improvement activities. This could result in a virtuous cycle of improvement leading to more free time, leading to more improvements, leading to more free time and so on.[9]

Alternatively, you could look around, can you help any other teams? Can you take up some work from other teams if they are under stress? Or, even better, can you help them improve and free up some of their time?

| 16 |

Inspiration 16: Cobra Chaos: When Solutions Bite Back!

Back in the colonial era, when the British ruled India, the British government introduced a program to reduce the population of cobras in Delhi. They were causing too many deaths in this highly populated region, and something had to be done. The program offered a bounty for dead cobras: Whoever killed one could take the dead cobra to the British officials and get paid for their effort.

Sounds straightforward, right? Certainly not rocket science. It was a simple problem that called for a simple solution. But not quite!

Soon after the bounty was introduced, the enterprising Delhiites started breeding cobras – lots of cobras. Then, they would kill them and take them to the British officials for the bounty.

Realising their mistake, the British officials did the sensible thing and shut down the program.

Well, they were wrong again!

With no more bounties offered, there was no point in breeding and keeping the snakes, so the breeders released them. The end result: a spike in the population of cobras in Delhi.

This is called the "cobra effect": When an attempted solution to a problem makes the problem worse.

Sometimes, the negative impact of a solution is far broader than just making the problem worse. Let's do a thought experiment together. Imagine a large company where the board is putting significant pressure on the CEO to increase profits. Major shareholders are urgently demanding additional dividends, and the CEO has to find a way to increase profits. If the CEO can't increase profit, she will not get her bonus and, even worse, may lose her job.

Well, what is profit? It's revenue less cost. So, she simply has to increase revenues and/or decrease costs. Again, it sounds reasonably straightforward, right? She just has to figure out who in the company is generating revenue and who is generating costs.

Again, this isn't rocket science. In this company, revenue is generated by the sales department and the largest expenses are generated by the large software solutions department. So, the solution is simple: Hire more salespeople and reduce the workforce in software. Those IT guys are always late, anyway, and never deliver anything!

Our CEO goes ahead with the plan. Six months later, the larger sales team is bringing in more revenue, and the downsized software solutions department has reduced costs. Profits are going through the roof. The board is happy, shareholders are happy, and the CEO gets a big bonus. She can now buy that luxury boat she's always wanted.

Let's fast forward another six months. The under-resourced and overwhelmed software solutions team now has to manage and deliver on an influx of new projects while client requests from the sales team are impossible to keep up with. A growing number of projects are delayed and over budget. Unhappy clients are screaming at them. A few key people in the organisation resign and move to their competitors. All hell is breaking loose! You get the picture.

The sheer number of undelivered projects, poor quality, unhappy clients, talent churn, and lawsuits have forced the company to announce a major restructuring. The CEO is fired, and many people lose their jobs. Millions of dollars are wasted. And worst of all for the CEO: Her reputation has been ruined. She will never again get a decent senior leadership position. She can't afford to pay her big mortgage, let alone the payments on that luxury boat she purchased last year, and she will soon be filing for bankruptcy.

This was an intense and exaggerated thought experiment, but it illustrates how decisions that look like solutions can cause disastrous consequences. In both of the examples above, we were dealing with complex systems. And when we try to solve problems in complex systems, we need to engage "systems thinking".

Systems thinking basically means taking a step back and taking a holistic view of a system. It means that rather than looking at a system from the component view, you look at it as a whole. Systems thinking is about seeing the entire ecosystem, not just the organism.

The term 'system' in systems thinking is vital. By system, we mean a set of components working together in interconnected networks that make up a complex whole. Examples of systems include a software solution, the human body, the digestive system, a team, an organisation, and an ecosystem.

Individual systems are often components of a bigger system. For example, humans are components of a team; the team is a component of an organisation; the organisation is a component of society; society is a component of the entire earth's ecosystem. Earth is part of the solar system, which is part of the Milky Way galaxy, which is part of the universe, which is part of the multiverse, which is part of the... who knows what! There is always a bigger system.

Systems thinking is a paradigm, a problem-solving approach, and a worldview. It enables us to see the bigger picture and make decisions that not only address immediate problems but also have a lasting positive impact across time and space. Learning systems thinking is key to becoming wiser and making wiser decisions.

| 17 |

Inspiration 17: Five-Minute Solutions!

In the previous inspiration, we delved into the story of the cobra effect, where the British officials' solutions to the cobra problem in Delhi inadvertently led to an increase in the cobra population. This story was a classic example of a lack of systems thinking when dealing with complex problems. The officials failed to foresee how the system might react to their solution, which was introducing a bounty to manage the cobra population.

To come up with the most effective solution, we must understand the interconnected web of cause and effect within a system so that we can predict how the system might respond to our interventions. Imagine, hypothetically, that the British officials had succeeded in eradicating all the cobras; what might have been the unintended consequences?

For instance, if cobras primarily feed on rodents, a decrease in the cobra population could lead to a surge in the rat and mouse population, potentially resulting in a rodent plague. In fact, we know that pit vipers, which pose a significant threat to humans, are a food source for cobras. Thus, a reduction in the cobra population could lead to an increase in pit vipers.

However, when dealing with complex problems, there's a crucial step we need to take before even formulating a solution. And that is understanding the problem. In complex problem-solving, our initial step should be to develop a deep and detailed understanding of the problem at hand.

This is precisely where the British officials failed when addressing the cobra issue in early 19th-century India. They believed the problem to be the number of cobras. However, the real issue was something else. What is wrong with a large number of cobras living in an area with a high human population? It is not merely the presence of the snakes but the resulting bites that inflict injury or death upon people. Thus, the officials were, in reality, dealing with a public health issue: the fatalities and injuries caused by cobra bites, rather than an overabundance of cobras per se. These represent two subtly distinct problems.

Once we correctly define the problem, devising a solution often becomes straightforward. In this case, it's clear that a significant part of the solution would involve developing antivenom for cobras. Interestingly, the antivenom for cobras was developed a while after this incident. Other aspects of the solution might include educational programs on dealing with cobras and distributing protective equipment to communities.

Albert Einstein famously said, "If I had an hour to solve a problem, I'd spend 55 minutes thinking about the problem and five minutes thinking about solutions." This quote encapsulates the importance of thoroughly understanding a problem before attempting to solve it.

| 18 |

Inspiration 18: The Blowback!

In 2018, there was a major scandal in Australia involving Victoria state police faking breathalyser results. The police apparently had quotas to fill, which motivated officers to blow into breathalysers themselves multiple times to meet the quotas. Over a period of a few years, more than a quarter million breath tests were faked by the Victoria police.

I remember I was driving one morning and listening to a morning radio show with the well-known ABC host Jon Faine (Jon was an incredible radio host and a great journalist, but not a systems thinker). Jon was interviewing the police commissioner and scrutinising him over this scandal. I remember clearly Jon was asking with an angry voice, "So who is going to lose their job over this scandal?" And I yelled back at the radio in my car, "No, Jon. Replacing people won't make the slightest difference. The problem is not the person; it's the quotas. Even if you fire the person in charge and hire another one, they will make the exact same mistake. This behaviour is what the job requires from them."

In this story, Jon fell victim to a bias called "fundamental attribution error" (also known as the "correspondence bias"). The fundamental attribution error is a tendency to explain someone's behaviour based on the person's internal characteristics, such as their personality, skills, experience, or disposition, rather than external factors, such as rules, processes, or operating environments. This bias is quite common in the business world. When things go wrong, we tend to blame the person in charge.

In most cases, however, it's not a person to be blamed but "the system" that promotes certain types of behaviour. Said differently, regardless of my personality, values, and characteristics, I will be more likely to behave according to what my environment rewards me or penalises me for.

This concept is brilliantly articulated by W. Edwards Deming, "People are already doing their best. The problem is with the system". Deming also famously said, "A bad system will beat a good person every time." By "system" here, we refer to the broader ecosystem in which we operate. The system encompasses the org structure, the processes and procedures, bonus structure, KPIs, job descriptions of various roles, the political environment within the organisation, what people are rewarded or penalised for, official and unofficial communication channels, information silos, and so on.

I invite you to think about what it is in the "System" that promotes unhelpful behaviours in your team. And what can you do to change the system?

Is this true?	Who did it	
Outcome	Myself	Someone Else
Positive	Personality	Circumstances
Negative	Circumstances	Personality

| 19 |

Inspiration 19: Think Small, Think Big!

In this inspiration, we explore the two main paradigms of reasoning in science: Analysis and Synthesis. To become a better systems thinker, it is essential to understand the differences between analysis and synthesis.

Analysis is a method of reasoning whereby we try to understand a system by breaking it down into its constituent components and understanding the properties of those components.

By comparison, synthesis works in the reverse direction. Synthesis is a method of reasoning whereby we try to understand a component of a system through the context of its relationships within the whole system.

If you want to solve a problem using analysis, you have to first break down the problem into sub-problems. Solve those sub-problems, and then put those solutions back together to solve the whole. But if you are trying to solve a problem using synthesis, you have to first identify the broader ecosystem that your problem is part of and try to solve your problem by gaining an understanding of the relationships of your problem with other elements of the broader ecosystem.

Russell Ackoff, one of the greatest systems thinkers of the 20th century, provides us with a great example that illustrates this. If you are trying to understand how a car's steering wheel mechanism works, you need to use analysis. You need to break down the steering wheel into its components, i.e., gears, shafts, and joints, and once you understand how these components and subsystems work, you'll know how the steering wheel works.

But if the problem you are trying to solve is to understand why the steering wheel is on the right side of the car in Australia and on the left side of the car in the United States, analysis will be futile. It doesn't matter how much you analyse the steering wheel; your answer is not in the car, and you will only confuse yourself by breaking down the steering wheel and looking at its components. To solve this problem, you need to apply synthesis, as the answer lies in understanding the broader ecosystem that the car is part of, that is, the transport system and its history.

Systems thinking typically requires more application of synthesis rather than analysis. When dealing with complex problems, we typically have to take a step back and look at the big picture. Synthesis helps us better understand the whole and build an "outside-in perspective".

In systems thinking we use synthesis

Analysis

Decompose a system to its elements

Understand the elements of the system

Roll up that understanding to understand the system

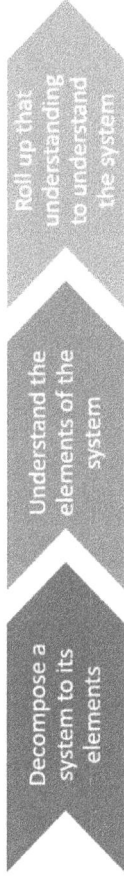

Related to Reductionism

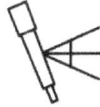

Synthesis

Identify the whole that the system is part of

Understand the relationships of the elements of the whole

Understand the system by understanding how it behaves in its ecosystem

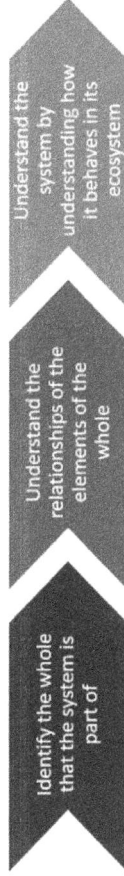

Related to Emergentism and Holism

| 20 |

Inspiration 20: Do What's Right, Not What's Easy!

The fourth law of systems thinking by Peter Senge[10] states, "The easy way out usually leads back in". This law is referring to the fact that we often find comfort in applying familiar solutions to problems, sticking to what we know best. Let's delve into an intriguing story that demonstrates this concept.

In the 1950s, the World Health Organisation (WHO) decided to ramp up the use of DDT worldwide in an attempt to control and even possibly eradicate malaria. Previous success in controlling malaria using DDT in prior years was a strong indication for the WHO that eradication of malaria is a possibility. So, this was WHO's familiar solution, their easy solution. Soon after this widespread use of DDT in the 50s, the unforeseen consequences of this solution started to become apparent. In the following years, extensive research and inquiries were conducted into the environment and various communities impacted by DDT use.

We now have numerous examples of how DDT resulted in completely unforeseen side effects. I'd like to share two examples of how this easy way out (i.e., using DDT to control malaria) led right back in.

Story 1:

After DDT spraying in British Guiana, the mosquito species responsible for malaria transmission in humans was successfully exterminated. However, two other species of mosquito that fed primarily on animals survived the spraying. The subsequent reduction in malaria cases contributed to a 68% increase in the human population in the following years. This, in turn, led to an increase in land used for rice cultivation, leaving less land available for cattle farming. With the loss of cattle, those mosquito species that primarily fed on cattle switched to drawing blood from humans, resulting in an increase in the prevalence of malaria again. Thus, the familiar solution worked in the short term but led them back to the initial problem after a while.[11]

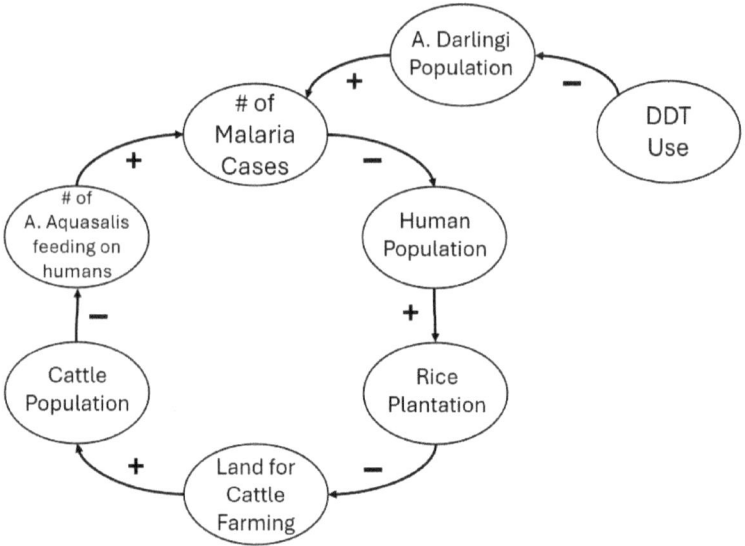

Law 4. The easy way out usually leads back in

Truly effective solutions often require fundamentally different approaches

Story 2:

Numerous reports suggest that the use of DDT has indirectly led to the death of household cats, which in turn resulted in an increase in the number of rodents in those communities. An investigation conducted in 1965 determined that, in one instance, an outbreak of Bolivian haemorrhagic fever was "due to the invasion of houses by rodents," a consequence of cat deaths following the spraying of DDT.[12]

Once again, resorting to the easy and familiar solution led to new, similar problems.

According to Peter Senge, *Truly effective solutions often require fundamentally different approaches.* So today, I challenge you to look at your work and identify areas where you are doing the easy thing instead of the right thing.

| 21 |

Inspiration 21: A Smart Heart!

I'd like you to close your eyes and think of someone who inspires you, who puts you at ease when you're near them. Someone who emanates positive energy, who is wise and calm even in the most turbulent situations. Who is this person? What is their name?

Such a person has high emotional intelligence. Simply put, Emotional Intelligence (EI) is the ability to recognise your own emotions and those of others. And to be able to manage and influence your own emotions and those of others. We make many decisions not with our cognitive capability but with our emotions. Mastering emotions will thus help us to become better decision-makers and enable us to influence others to make better decisions.

Some people say emotional intelligence is nothing more than a fancy term for manipulation. That is very far from the truth.

Did Martin Luther King "manipulate" people into supporting the civil rights movement? How about Nelson Mandela? Did he "manipulate" anyone into following him in his struggles against apartheid? No. They spoke with inspiration, passion, and courage, knowing the hearts of those who were listening, letting them decide.

How about the person you brought to mind earlier? The one who gives you a sense of calm and steadiness. Did he/she ever manipulate you into doing something? Or did they inspire and influence you? There is a big difference between manipulating someone into making a decision or influencing them into making that decision. Politicians manipulate; real leaders influence and inspire.

One of most popular models of EI is the "12 competency model" introduced by Daniel Goleman[13]. These 12 competencies are categorised in 4 domains.

Self-Awareness

1. **Emotional Self-Awareness:** The ability to understand our own emotions and their effects on our performance.

Self-Management

1. **Emotional Self-Control:** The ability to keep disruptive emotions and impulses in check and maintain our effectiveness under stressful or hostile conditions.

2. **Achievement Orientation:** Striving to meet or exceed a standard of excellence; looking for ways to do things better, set challenging goals, and take calculated risks.

3. **Positive Outlook:** The ability to see the positive in people, situations, and events and persistence in pursuing goals despite obstacles and setbacks.

4. **Adaptability:** Flexibility in handling change, juggling multiple demands, and adapting our ideas or approaches.

Social Awareness

1. **Empathy:** The ability to sense others' feelings and perspectives, taking an active interest in their concerns and picking up cues about what others feel and think.

2. **Organisational Awareness:** The ability to read a group's emotional currents and power relationships; identifying influencers, networks, and organisational dynamics.

Relationship Management

1. **Influence:** The ability to have a positive impact on others, persuading or convincing others in order to gain their support.

2. **Coach and Mentor:** The ability to foster the long-term learning or development of others by giving feedback, guidance, and support.

3. **Conflict Management:** The ability to help others through emotional or tense situations, tactfully bringing

disagreements into the open and finding solutions all can endorse.

4. **Inspirational Leadership:** The ability to inspire and guide individuals and groups towards a meaningful vision of excellence, and to bring out the best in others.

5. **Teamwork:** The ability to work with others towards a shared goal; participating actively, sharing responsibility and rewards, and contributing to the capability of the team.

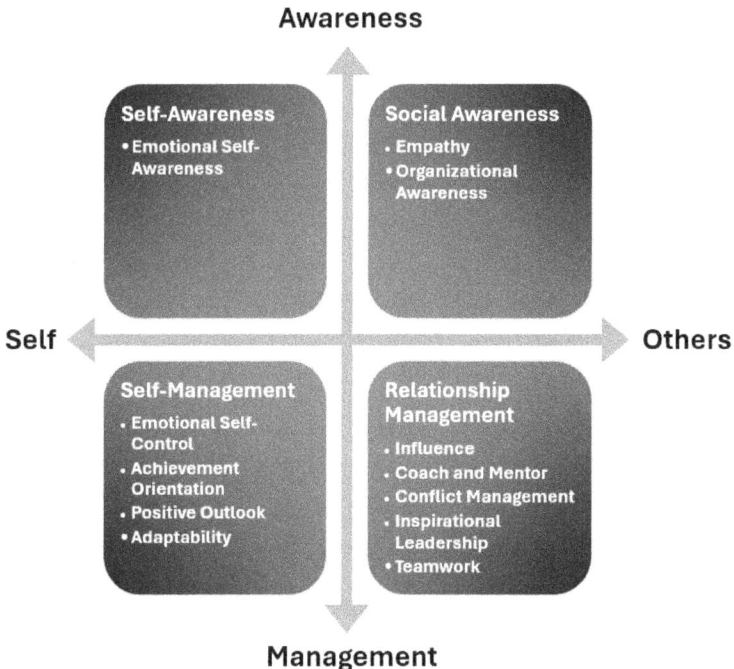

It may seem that these competencies are natural gifts that some people are born with. However, the truth is that Emotional Intelligence (EI) competencies can be developed by anyone through training and practice. While some individuals may have a higher natural disposition and find learning these skills easier, anyone can cultivate them. Just as height might be an advantage in volleyball, it isn't a definitive factor for success - there are numerous successful volleyball players who aren't particularly tall.

There's a wealth of resources available, including articles, books, and courses, to aid in developing EI competencies. In future inspirations, I will share techniques to further develop your emotional intelligence competencies.

| 22 |

Inspiration 22: The Vulcan Mind Meld!

One of the most fundamental emotional and social competencies is empathy. Empathy is a building block for other social and emotional skills. People skilled at empathy can connect with others better, they are better team players, and can better influence and inspire others.

I define empathy simply as "one's ability to experience the world through someone else's reality". Each person has their own distinct personality, life experience, beliefs, and sensations. The same event will thus be experienced differently depending on who you are. We all live in our own version of reality and can never truly experience another's, but we can get closer to it.

Empathy, then, is seeing the world through *their* eyes. Feeling their emotions; intuiting their sensations; understanding how their life experiences have shaped their character and perspective; experiencing their biases, motivations, and fears; and so on.

Most of the time when people think they are being empathetic, they are actually experiencing something called *projection*. Projection is when we put ourselves in the other person's shoes and think, what would *I* do or feel if I were in their position?

To give you an example, let's say someone is telling you a sad story about something that happened to them and they are grieving. As you *empathise* with their experience, you may think you are feeling their sadness, but you are probably experiencing how you *imagine* their sadness feels, not how it really is. So in this sense you are projecting yourself into their reality. You are attempting to understand how the event would have felt to *you* instead of how the event would have felt to them.

True empathy is trying to understand how an event feels to someone who is essentially quite different from you. Genuine empathy is not only understanding what is going on in their heads but also connecting to what is going on in their hearts and feeling their emotions as they feel it. And to be able to empathise with someone you need to be genuinely curious, care for them as human being, connect with them on a deep level, let go of yourself and fully tune into them.

Empathy is incredibly powerful. It will bring you much wisdom. In "seeing through other people's eyes", it will be as if you have lived multiple lives!

Experience the world through someone else's reality

Don't put yourself in their shoes
Different beliefs, personality, values, objectives

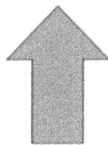

Be Curiosity
Place full attention and focus on them

Understand their mind and heart as they are, not as how you would think and feel in their position!

| 23 |

Inspiration 23: The Goldilocks Zone: Not Too Hot, Not Too Cold!

The Yerkes–Dodson law, a well-known concept in psychology, illustrates how our performance is correlated with the level of stress hormones in our bodies. At low levels, we're relaxed, but our focus on tasks is minimal. Tasks undertaken in this state are often performed automatically, like driving, or may even feel a little boring.

As our arousal, and consequently our stress hormone levels, rise, so does our performance, peaking at what psychologists call the 'Flow' state. This state of maximal cognitive efficiency and maximum neural harmony occurs when the challenge at hand matches your skill level, leading to full mental immersion and focus on the task. Time seems to fly by, and you may become so immersed in your task that you lose awareness of your surroundings.

However, stress hormones only enhance our performance up to a point. Beyond this, any further increase can lead to a decline in performance. When stress is excessive, we may become frazzled or enter a fight-or-flight mode.

Each of these states serves a purpose in different situations. The fully relaxed state is where our minds ideally spend half the day. This state is ideal for creative thinking, and innovative ideas are usually generated when you are in this state. The fully stressed state is beneficial when facing danger and needing to ensure our survival. And the Flow state is ideal when a task requires our full focus or when we need to solve a specific problem.

Often at work, we experience stress levels that exceed what is optimal for the situation. This is particularly true in high-pressure environments where delivery deadlines are tight. Ironically, this high pressure may push us beyond our peak performance range, resulting in further delays in delivery. So, to maximise our performance at work, it's essential that we arm ourselves with effective stress management techniques. Common mindfulness practices, such as slow deep breathing, various forms of meditation, and physical exercise, can effectively reduce stress levels. In future inspirations, I will delve into more techniques for stress reduction and management.

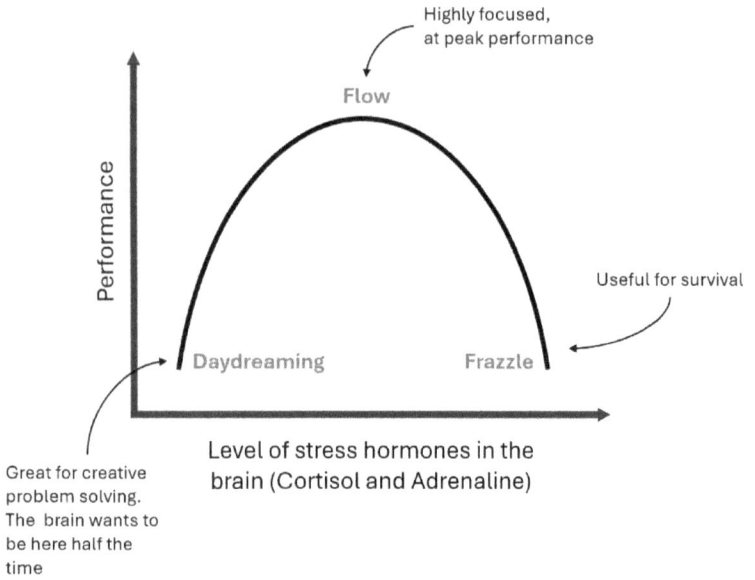

Highly focused, at peak performance

Flow

Performance

Useful for survival

Daydreaming

Frazzle

Level of stress hormones in the brain (Cortisol and Adrenaline)

Great for creative problem solving. The brain wants to be here half the time

| 24 |

Inspiration 24: Oops, We Did It Again!

Risk is defined by two factors: the probability of an event occurring and the impact of that event. Consider a large company like Meta, for instance, planning to introduce a new feature to their flagship product, Facebook. If something goes wrong during the release, it could potentially upset billions of users. In this scenario, the risk impact is quite high – if things go wrong, billions of users could be dissatisfied.

A simplistic view of risk management suggests that to avoid upsetting billions of users, the likelihood of errors and mishaps should be minimised. This involves rigorous design and extensive planning to anticipate every possible outcome and ensure flawless execution. This approach often leads to numerous sign-offs, approvals, red tape, and a waterfall approach to delivery. However, this method contradicts the agile delivery philosophy, which encourages a test-and-learn mindset and fosters a safe-to-fail environment. So, what's the alternative? How can Facebook foster creativity, innovation, and agility while managing risks when delivering complex solutions to billions of users?

Rather than focusing on reducing the likelihood, they concentrate on minimising the impact. They essentially create an environment where mistakes are acceptable. Instead of releasing new features to all users simultaneously, they initially release it to a small subset of users and then incrementally roll it out to the rest.

Today, I invite you to consider how you can minimise the impact of risks in your project. How can you foster an environment where taking risks and making mistakes is acceptable because the impact of those risks is small and manageable? This is not to suggest that we should entirely disregard reducing risk likelihood. Instead, we should prioritise minimising the impact first, and then reducing the risk likelihood.

High Probability
Low Impact

Low Probability
Low Impact

Low Probability
High Impact

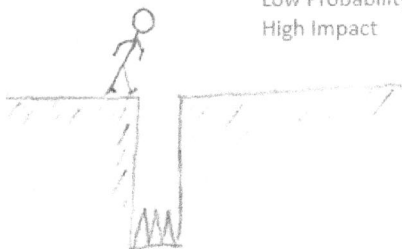

High Probability
High Impact

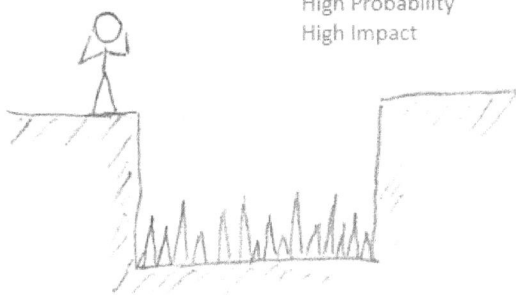

| 25 |

Inspiration 25: Zoom Out and Tune In!

One of the biggest impacts of the COVID-19 pandemic was accelerating the transition to remote work, which has both advantages and disadvantages. One of the main drawbacks of remote work is Zoom fatigue and a decrease in communication quality.

In this inspiration, I offer three simple tips to enhance the quality of our remote meetings.

The 25/50 Rule

Due to remote working conditions, back-to-back meetings have become more frequent. When we are in the office, having back-to-back meetings is not a big issue, as moving between rooms for meetings provides short breaks that refresh us and reset our minds. However, working from home often means transitioning from one Zoom meeting to another without leaving our desks.

To mitigate this, some companies have implemented the 25/50-minute rule for meetings. Instead of scheduling 30-minute meetings, they book 25-minute ones, and 50-minute meetings replace the typical hour-long ones. This strategy allows for short breaks between meetings to stretch, grab a quick drink, or take a bio break.

These 5-10 minute breaks can significantly enhance our productivity.

Notice the Unmute

In remote meetings, since we are not physically in the same room, it's more challenging to pick up on unspoken or visual cues. Therefore, we need to make a conscious effort to tune into each other during meetings.

If someone unmutes themselves during a remote meeting, it's likely an indication that they want to speak. If you notice this cue, it's good practice to give the unmuted person time to speak or call out their name and ask for their input.

Have Video On

Attending meetings with our videos off deprives our colleagues of crucial non-verbal cues. While this may not be a significant issue for everyone, many people find it challenging to communicate effectively without seeing the person they're talking to.

I've noticed that when I'm in a meeting where most attendees have their videos off, I tend to repeat myself and speak louder. Upon reflection, I realised that not seeing the eyes of the people I'm talking to or their nods of understanding, I subconsciously assume they haven't understood me.

Having videos on helps us see each other's emotions and fosters a more human connection. Another indirect benefit of having videos on is that it discourages multitasking and promotes focus on the ongoing conversation.

While there are situations where it's beneficial to have videos off (e.g., bandwidth issues), generally, making a conscious effort to have videos on when possible can significantly improve the productivity of our remote meetings.

3 SIMPLE TIPS TO MAKE ZOOM MEETINGS MORE FUN!

Reduce Zoom fatigue

Effective
Remote
Meetings

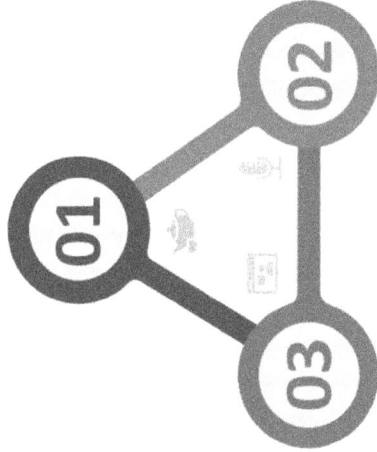

Have video on

Having video on helps others see your emotions. Having video off is disrespectful. It feels like you are hiding, you are multitasking or you are disengaged

The 25/50 rule

Instead of 30-minute meetings book 25-minute meetings. And instead of 1-hour meetings book 50-minute meetings

Notice the unmute

In remote meetings when someone unmutes themselves it is probably an indication that they would like to talk. Notice the cue and ask their opinion

| 26 |

Inspiration 26: Mirror, Mirror, in the Design!

Conway's Law states that "Organisations which design systems are constrained to produce designs which are copies of the communication structures of these organisations." This means the organisation's structure influences the architecture of the systems it produces.

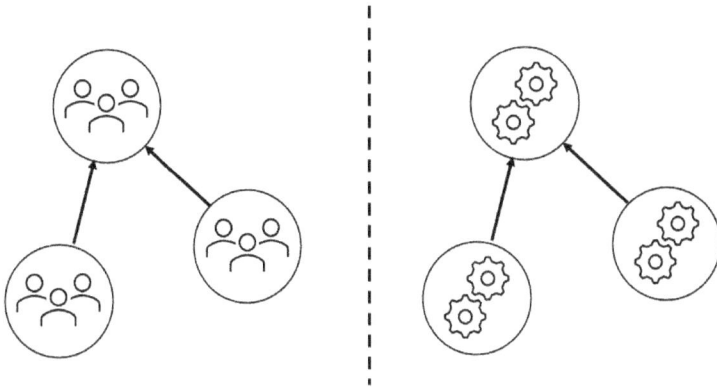

Here are three instances of Conway's Law in action:

Website UX:

Research done by UX expert Nigel Bevan[14] on corporate website design found that end-users often became frustrated with company websites because the navigation, page design, and content structure often mirrored the internal concerns of an organisation, instead of meeting the needs of the intended user first.

Tesla vs Chevy Bolt:

Chevy Bolt has three cooling systems: one for the battery, one for the cabin, and one for the electronics. Because there are different departments in charge of the battery pack, cabin, and electronics. On the other hand, the Tesla Model 3 has a single cooling system called the Superbottle that is responsible for cooling the entire car.

Amazon:

Back in the early days of Amazon, their front page was a 400 MB monolith binary, and it could take up to 12 hours to compile. Then, in the late 2000s, Jeff Bezos decided to break down the company structure into small teams. This facilitated the transition of the Amazon monolith to a few hundred micro-services, each of which was developed and maintained by one of those small teams.

Today, I invite you to reflect on how your organisation's communication structures are mirrored in your enterprise architecture, software solutions, products, and services.

| 27 |

Inspiration 27: Outside-in Perspective!

In his famous TED Talk, "Start with Why," Simon Sinek introduces the idea that "People don't buy what you do; they buy why you do it." In this video, Sinek underscores the importance of purpose for organisations.

One might wonder why some companies, like Apple, are more successful than others, despite their competitors having the same access to technologies, talent, and markets. Why did Martin Luther King lead the Civil Rights Movement while there were many other inspirational speakers who also suffered racial discrimination? Why were the Wright Brothers the first to achieve controlled powered flight, despite there being better-funded and technically competent teams working on the same problem? The answer lies in the leaders' ability to connect with their purpose. They started with 'why.' They knew their 'why,' and everything they did aligned with it.

Nowadays, every large corporation defines a purpose. However, most of the time, the purpose definition is more of a marketing endeavour than a mechanism to identify and connect with their 'why.'

Most companies fail to define inspirational purpose statements. Here are some examples of uninspiring purpose statements from actual companies in Australia:

A major bank:

"Shape a world where people and communities thrive."
Really? What does that have to do with banking?

A major telecom:

"We help businesses and people communicate anytime and in many ways."
Of course, you're a telecom company. Tell me the "why".

A major superannuation retirement fund:

"To help our members end up with more money in retirement."
Isn't that just the definition of a retirement fund? What is your "why"?

A major mining company:

"To bring people and resources together to build a better world."

What does that even mean? These are just some nice words clearly written by marketing consultants.

None of the above statements tell us why they do what they do.

In contrast, one of the best purpose statements I've ever seen is from another major superannuation retirement fund:

"Understand me, look after me, secure my future."

What makes this purpose statement exceptional, apart from the fact that it tells us why they do what they do, is that it's written in the first person from the client's point of view, not from the organisation's point of view. It acknowledges that the organisation has an external purpose: to serve someone.

In a purposeful organisation, everyone knows how their work contributes to the purpose of the organisation. A great example of this is Toyota. If you go to a Toyota factory and ask a worker what their job is, they won't say, "My job is to install a tyre," or "My job is to mount the seats," or "My job is to paint the car." They'll say, "I build Toyotas."

A purposeful organisation is one where people see the bigger picture and understand the connection between what they do and the organisation's purpose. In such an organisation, people don't see themselves as just a software engineer, a risk manager, or a customer service representative. They don't see themselves as a cog in the machine. They see themselves as providing exceptional products or services to the end client. And they can feel pride in the work they do.

So, how do you create a company where people know how they contribute? It's by developing an outside-in perspective. Our clients don't know about our various divisions, systems, policies, silos, or the technologies we use within the organisation. They just see the organisation as a whole. Our clients don't care about our internal challenges; they only care about receiving quality products and services.

Only when we adopt the outside-in perspective of our clients, can we understand and connect what we do in the organisation to why we do it. Ultimately, let's remember: "You can't read the label on a jar by being inside the jar!"

| 28 |

Inspiration 28: The Laws of Agile!

What we now refer to as "Agile" began in 2001 in the software development industry. Since then, this concept has evolved from a better way of delivering software to an organisation's ability to respond to change quickly and easily – or business agility.

According to management thought leader Steve Denning[15], agile organisations exhibit three key characteristics:

The law of the small team

Agile organisations are made up of small, autonomous, cross-functional teams that have the capability to deliver value end-to-end. These teams have the ability to get continuous feedback from their end clients directly. These small teams are empowered to do whatever they have to do to get the job done. They don't have to deal with bureaucracy and processes that don't add much value to the end client.

The law of the customer

Agile organisations are externally focussed rather than internally focussed. This is what we call "outside-in perspective". The clients see one black-box system, your organisation, but from the inside, we see the organisation's various departments, units, and systems. Customers don't care about our internal structure, systems, processes, and goals. Similarly, we need to look at our organisation from the customer's perspective.

In an agile organisation, everyone has a clear line of sight to the ultimate customer and can articulate how their work adds value to the end client – or not. If their work isn't adding value to the end client, then an immediate question arises as to why the work is being done at all.

The law of the network

In agile organisations, having small, autonomous, and cross-functional teams is insufficient if they operate within a broader bureaucratic structure. As organisations grow, hierarchies are inevitable. Hierarchies are needed to organise large numbers of people. However, these hierarchies often become dysfunctional when they shape how we communicate and collaborate. In agile organisations, teams collaborate and communicate across business units in an organic, network-like structure.

| 29 |

Inspiration 29: When Crowns Are Optional and Aprons Are Not!

The term "servant leadership" was introduced and popularised by management consultant Robert K. Greenleaf as an alternative to authoritarian leadership. Some people associate "leadership" with being in a position of authority, being "the boss". And they think that leaders are served by others in the same way that kings and feudal lords had servants to do their bidding. The servant-leader is the opposite of this. The servant-leader is here to serve, not be served.

Most great leaders from history were servant leaders. People like Mahatma Gandhi, Nelson Mandela, and Martin Luther King were great examples of servant leaders. They started with an urge to serve and then rose to lead. Famous religious figures were also servant leaders. Jesus, Muhammad, Moses, and

Buddha, among others, were the ultimate servant leaders. These are some of the most influential people of all time who left a mark on humanity so profound that they continue to shape us long after they've gone.

There are key differences between rank or authority and leadership. When you are in a position of authority, people *have* to obey you. But when you are a true leader, people *choose* to follow you because they are inspired. Dave Ramsey[16] describes the difference between leaders and bosses as "leaders pull while bosses push". If you are a leader, you will be at the front, showing people the way. But if you are a boss, you will sit behind the group, trying to manage and direct its movement.

I'm not saying that hierarchies are bad or we should get rid of them. Hierarchies do and must exist. But there's an important distinction to make: A hierarchy with a "leader" at the top will be highly functional. A hierarchy led by someone who is not a leader will be highly dysfunctional. In a functional hierarchy, the people at the top of the pyramid are leaders. They will enjoy the perks of their position, but they have a duty; they are there to serve. The duty of leaders is to serve those with less power.

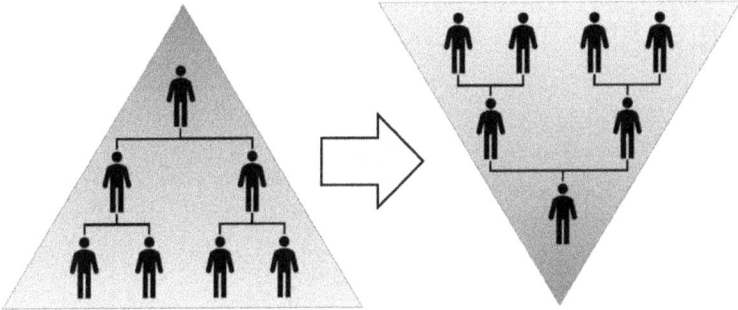

"The servant-leader is servant first... It begins with the natural feeling that one wants to serve, to serve first. Then conscious choice brings one to aspire to lead. That person is sharply different from one who is leader first."

—ROBERT K. GREENLEAF

| 30 |

Inspiration 30: Influential, Not Influencer!

Influence is the ability to positively impact others, persuading or convincing them to gain their support. Some argue that our emotions play a more crucial role in decision-making than cognitive reasoning. So, to influence someone effectively, we must appeal to their emotions. Influence rests on two pillars: empathy and integrity.

Using empathy to appeal to the self-interest of others

In order to influence others, we need to appeal to their self-interest. We must first consider "What's in it for them?" and then anticipate the questions they may have.

So, to influence someone, we first have to understand them. What are their motives and values? What do they care about? To answer these questions, we need to be empathetic. Empathy will help us understand what matters to them and to see the world from their perspective. But we have to be careful because if we get it wrong, we will lose their trust. If we practise projection rather than empathy, it could lead to reducing our influence rather than increasing it.

We can't think for others and assume we know what's in their best interest. It's not about us. We have to genuinely care for their "needs" and "wants" and see the world through their lens. Our perception is our reality, and their perception is their reality. To be effective in the art of influence, your message must be aligned with their perception of the world, not yours. And the best way to do this is to come from the heart and truly care about their objectives and self-interests.

How to influence without manipulating

Have you ever had a boss who made promises that they didn't keep? How did that make you feel? A common tactic when people try to influence others is not being fully transparent and disclosing information selectively. These tactics may work in the short term but are disastrous in the long term.

Some people call these tactics Machiavellian – secretly manipulative. It's why we don't trust politicians. Whenever you use such methods, you set yourself up for failure. We are in a 21st-century corporate environment; people are smart and will figure out what's happening soon enough. Then they will lose trust and you will become the object of their discontent.

So, as leaders, we need to make sure we stick to our words, are transparent, and don't provide information selectively to imply things that are not true. We must be vigilant in ensuring we aren't manipulating others and be very careful about what we promise.

To illustrate this, let's compare two of the most famous leaders in history, Joseph Stalin and Nelson Mandela. Both leaders were highly successful, yet one was manipulative and the other was inspiring. They have both left a lasting impact on a global scale, though we love one while we despise the other. The difference between these two leaders was that Nelson Mandela wanted what was in the best interest of his people, but Joseph Stalin wanted what was in his own best interest.

When a leader uses his/her empathy and emotional intelligence without integrity, he/she becomes manipulative. But when emotional intelligence and empathy are used with integrity the leader becomes influential and inspirational.

How to supercharge your influence

There are other qualities that enhance our influencing capability, such as charisma, charm, and powerful allies. However, without empathy and integrity, these factors are ineffective. For instance, having a robust network of influential friends can boost your influence. But if you leverage that network without integrity or empathy, your reputation may suffer, and you'll be perceived as a shifty politician.

To supercharge our influence, we must combine charm, charisma, and powerful allies with a core foundation rooted in empathy and integrity.

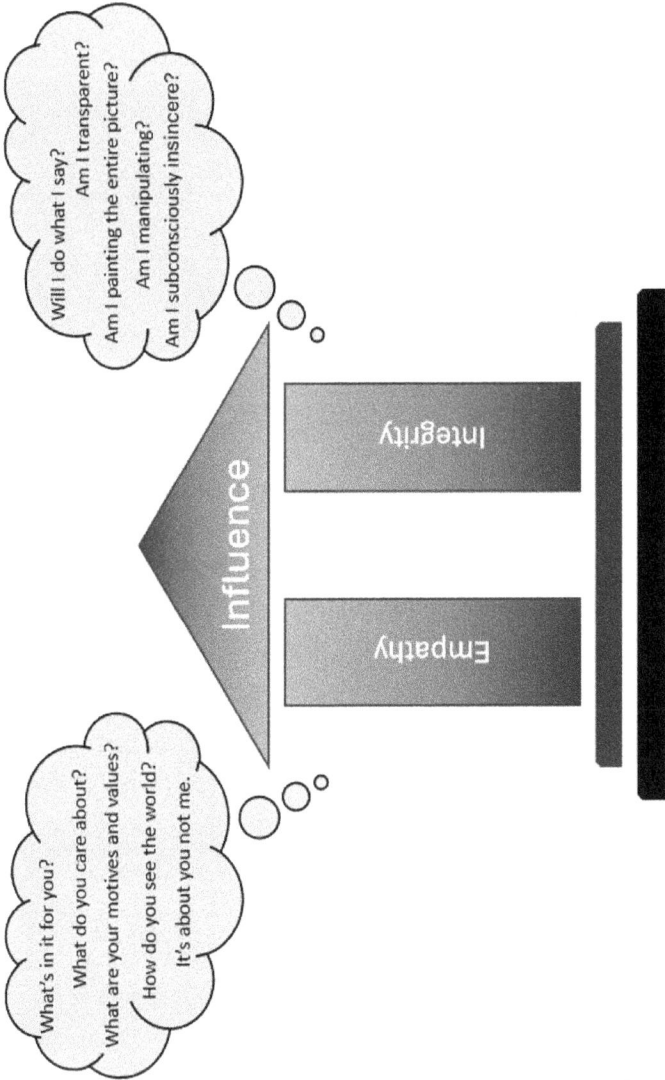

Will I do what I say?
Am I transparent?
Am I painting the entire picture?
Am I manipulating?
Am I subconsciously insincere?

Influence

Integrity

Empathy

What's in it for you?
What do you care about?
What are your motives and values?
How do you see the world?
It's about you not me.

| 31 |

Inspiration 31: The Dolphins Under the Iceberg!

One of the critical competencies of great leaders is *coaching*. Like many other words in English, coaching means different things to different people. A coach could mean anything from an instructor, trainer, and mentor to a consultant, guide, and even a guru. But none of these words describe the real meaning of coaching.

The International Coaching Federation (ICF) defines coaching as "partnering with clients in a thought-provoking and creative process that inspires them to maximise their personal and professional potential." A coach does not teach you how to do things, give advice, tell you the answer, or show you the way; the coach only facilitates your thinking process.

To better understand this, let's use the metaphor of an iceberg to describe the different types of internal obstacles that we may face in order to achieve our goals. Above the surface, we have things like skills and knowledge. Below the surface, we have values, self-image, traits, and motives. Coaching is a tool that is used to remove the impediments that are below the surface.

Teaching and consulting, by comparison, work above the surface. Teaching involves modelling, guiding practice, observing practice, and giving performance feedback. It's appropriate when someone has a skill or knowledge gap.

We are consulting when we ask guiding questions, give advice, and co-create. It's appropriate when someone needs a thinking partner to solve a problem. Coaching is about helping someone uncover their internal obstacles to achieving success and learn how to manage them. It's appropriate when we realise that skill and knowledge gaps are not the primary obstacle to high performance.

I'd like to make a subtle point here: A coach should not bring his/her opinion into the conversation. I remember when I was learning how to coach. Sometimes, my client would present a problem, and I knew exactly what he needed to do to fix the issue. The solution was crystal clear – for me. But as soon as I started leaking solutions or asking loaded questions, my mentor would stop me and say that I was no longer coaching.

Remember, in the inspiration about empathy, we discussed the fact that each of us has different life experiences, views, and perceptions. These differences become even more prominent when we bring in values, self-image, traits, and motives. These characteristics are deeply interrelated with who we are.

When coaching, you should not provide answers; you should simply use empathy to facilitate the thinking process of the person you are coaching, helping them find their own solution—a solution that may be wildly different from what you had in mind.

Also, it is essential **not** to ask loaded or rhetorical questions to guide the person you are coaching to where you think the answer is. If you have an opinion, you can put it on the table and teach them or offer consultation. To coach effectively and remove those impediments that are under the surface, all you need to do is ask open-ended questions with genuine curiosity. People often drive with their handbrakes engaged, and your role as a coach is to help them identify those handbrakes and release them.

Easier to see and develop

Necessary for top performance but not sufficient

Skills

Knowledge

Values

Self-Image

Traits

Motives

Characteristics that lead to longer term success

Harder to see and develop

Teaching
- Is when we model, guide practice, observe practice and give performance feedback.
- Is appropriate when someone has a skill or knowledge gap.

Consulting
- Is asking guiding questions, giving advice, and co-creating.
- Is appropriate when someone needs a thought partner to help solve problems.

Coaching
- Is supporting someone to uncover their internal obstacles and to learn how to manage them
- Is appropriate when we realise that skill and knowledge gaps are not the primary obstacle to performance.

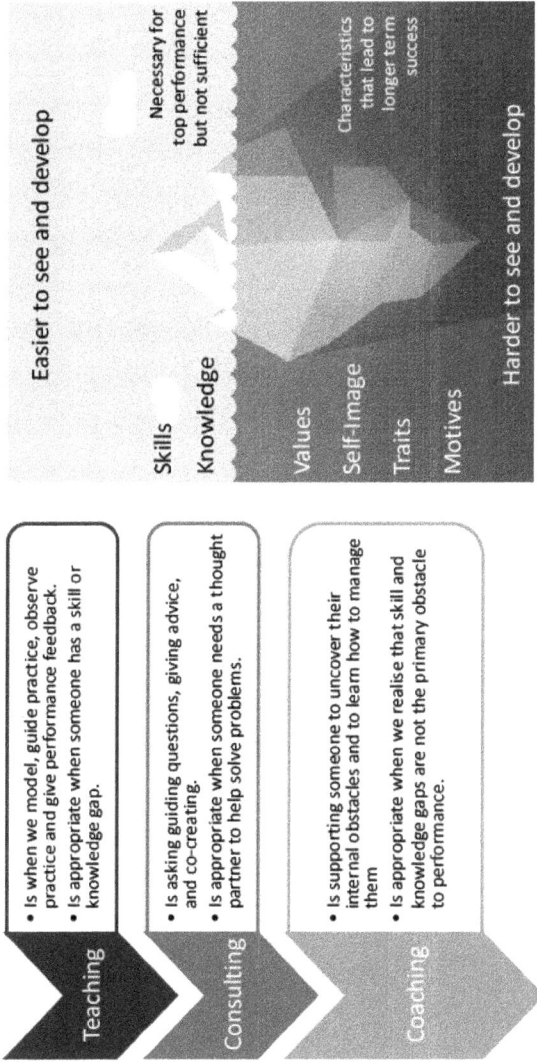

Coaching, consulting, and teaching distinctions by Matthew Taylor and Daniel Goleman

| 32 |

Inspiration 32: Resistance Is Futile!

Contrary to popular belief, people do not inherently resist change. Resistance often arises in the context of organisational change, not due to the change itself, but rather the uncertainty that accompanies it. Ironically, most of the time, people love change when they do not feel threatened. Intrinsically, our brains are receptive to change!

The human brain is hardwired for curiosity and exploration, yet it also maintains a level of caution towards the unknown. The emotions we experience in the face of uncertainty serve as protective mechanisms, ensuring our survival.

However, these same emotions that exist to protect us can sometimes hold us hostage, preventing us from contributing positively to change.

For an organisational transformation initiative to be successful, we need the people involved to embrace the change and provide positive, creative, and innovative contributions. This is only achievable if those individuals feel safe.

As leaders, we can enhance our effectiveness by fostering an environment of safety and trust for our teams. This can be achieved by minimising uncertainty and maximising transparency. Similarly, those impacted by change can increase their effectiveness by focusing on the positive aspects of change, rather than the negatives.

It's a myth that people resist change
Our brains love change inherently.

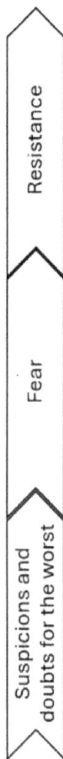

Human brain is wired to be curious and want to explore new things.

Suspicions and doubts for the worst → Fear → Resistance

We resist when our curiosity is held hostage by defensiveness and fear.

Environment of Safety and Trust → Less Fear → Focus on the positive → jump on the bandwagon → Contribute innovatively → Better outcomes

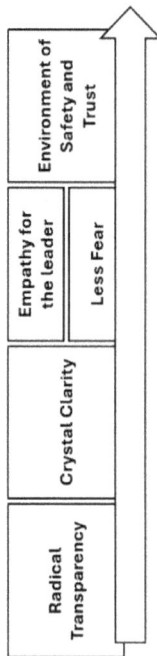

Radical Transparency	Crystal Clarity	Empathy for the leader	Environment of Safety and Trust
		Less Fear	

Example technique
Speed Dating
Once a week for half a day leader book 30-minute blocks to have 1:1 with team members

BASED ON THE WORKS OF GEORGE KOHLRIESER & DANIEL GOLEMAN

| 33 |

Inspiration 33: A Leadership Superpower!

Listening is one of the most powerful competencies of great leaders. If leaders were superheroes, listening would be their superpower because it enables them to build strong alliances and make effective decisions.

The concept of listening as a leadership superpower extends beyond active listening. It begins at the foundation, which involves altering the intent behind listening. For listening to become a superpower, your intention must be to understand, not to convince.

Your mindset shapes your intent behind listening. If your mindset is, "I know the answers; I just have to convince others to follow my lead," then your intention for listening will be to convince rather than understand. Consequently, while listening, you'll be formulating arguments in your head to persuade the other person.

In this scenario, you are listening to respond, not to understand. You become defensive as you think about how to prove your point, which may prevent you from deeply understanding the other person.

Often at work, our conversations involve complex topics, requiring active cooperation between the speaker and listener to convey critical points. If the listener isn't actively trying to understand, they may miss essential data points. As a result, they may not form a holistic perspective or foresee the consequences of their decisions, leading to poor or suboptimal decision-making.

Furthermore, the speaker may feel unheard, reducing their trust in the leader.

On the other hand, if your intent is to listen to understand and you practice active listening, you can better comprehend the complexities and nuances of the conversation. This leads to a more holistic understanding of the situation and an improved ability to predict unforeseen consequences of decisions, resulting in better decision-making.

Moreover, people will feel heard, and the leader's trust and credibility increase.

How to Use Listening as a Superpower:

- Listen carefully with a genuine intention to understand the other person's perspective when they are speaking.
- Avoid formulating a reply in your mind or thinking about how to convince them.

- Refrain from interrupting until they've finished making their point.
- After they've finished, pause. If you disagree with them, you can express it now. Alternatively, you can tell them you'll consider their views and get back to them.

Some of us may have been frequently interrupted or had our views dismissed in our careers. To protect ourselves, we may feel the need to be loud and interrupt others; otherwise, we won't get anywhere. However, not listening won't get us any-where either. There are many techniques we can use to assert ourselves and ensure our voices are heard, but interrupting others isn't one of them.

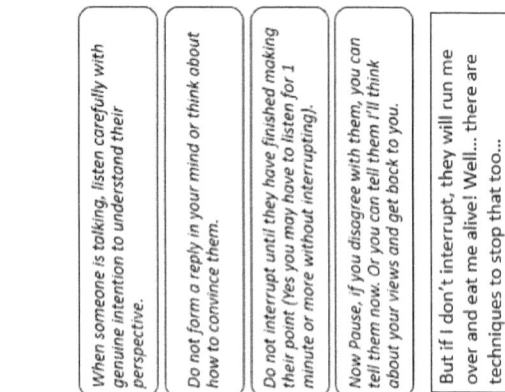

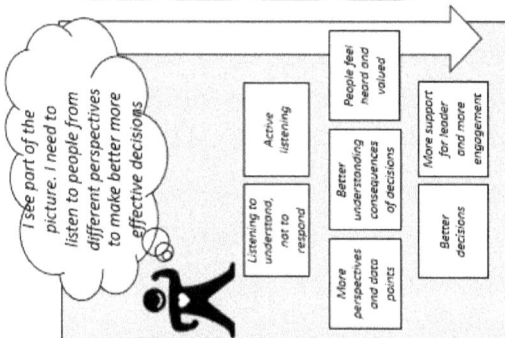

| 34 |

Inspiration 34: Leadership in Full Colour!

Some of us may find it challenging to work with colleagues who disagree with us. We may avoid them or wish we didn't have to work with them. But in fact, it is a blessing to have thoughtful people around us who disagree with us.

Ray Dalio, the American billionaire investor and the founder of Bridgewater, talks about the concept of thoughtful disagreement in his book, *Principles: Life and Work.* As the leader of Bridgewater, Dalio intentionally surrounds himself with thoughtful people who disagree with him. This expands his thinking and opens him up to new perspectives of seeing the world.

"What I wanted most from them was thoughtful disagreement … Going from seeing things through just my eyes to seeing things through the eyes of these thoughtful people was like going from seeing things in black and white to seeing them in colour. The world lit up."
— RAY DALIO

If we keep an open mind, seek disagreement, and bring together concepts and ideas from a diversity of views, we will have a clearer, more colourful, and a richer view of reality.

Great leaders welcome "Thoughtful Disagreement."

Inspiration 35: How Do You Know You're Right?

Empiricism, the foundation of the scientific method, is an approach to problem-solving that involves viewing our solutions with scepticism and only accepting them as true when we observe validated evidence.

To illustrate this, let's consider a story. Legend has it that in the 17th century, young Isaac Newton was sitting under an apple tree in the English countryside. At that time, a plague epidemic had caused universities to close for two years, sending students home. Back at his countryside residence, Newton was studying the motion of celestial bodies, trying to understand what makes the moon orbit the Earth.

While pondering this problem under the apple tree, an apple suddenly fell. This sparked an epiphany: perhaps the same force pulling the apple to the ground was also causing the moon to orbit the Earth.

This was a moment of insight, and his intuition was telling him this must be true, but he knew he couldn't simply accept this conjecture as truth. He needed to validate it. After conducting several experiments, Newton formulated his famous gravity equation. This equation made numerous predictions, from the movement of celestial bodies to the trajectory a ball would follow when thrown at a certain velocity. After meticulously measuring the predictions of his hypothesis, Newton gained enough confidence to believe his hypothesis was true.

This story illustrates empiricism in action. In today's uncertain world, business and technology professionals need to apply an empirical approach to validate their ideas. One way to validate our hypotheses is by building MVPs.

MVP, or Minimum Viable Product, is often misunderstood as the smallest and quickest-to-build version of a product that delivers value to customers. However, the true definition of an MVP is the smallest, quickest-to-build version of a product that allows us to gain insight and validate our hypothesis.

In the words of Eric Ries, the author of The Lean Startup, "The minimum viable product is that version of a new product a team uses to collect the maximum amount of validated learning about customers with the least effort."

We don't build the MVP to deliver value to our customers. We build it to learn and validate our hypothesis. There's another concept, MMP (Minimal Marketable Product), which is the smallest iteration of our product that delivers value to our customers.

A team may build multiple MVPs before they build their first MMP. Or, their first MVP may actually be the MMP. Delivering customer value is crucial, and no business survives without it. However, the step before delivering value is learning. So, when designing MVPs, we need to ask ourselves:

1. What is it that we are trying to learn by building this MVP?
2. What is the hypothesis we are validating?
3. How will we measure and gather data, and how will that data provide us with insight?

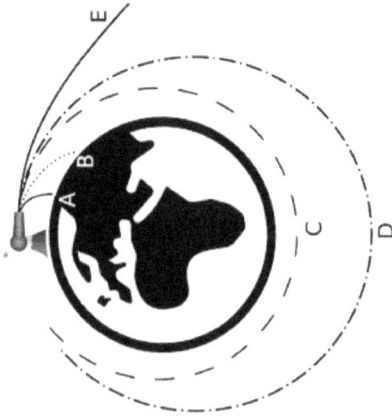

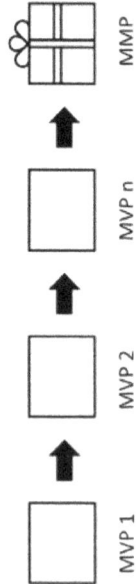

| 36 |

Inspiration 36: The Serious Business of Being Silly!

People respond to stressful situations in various ways. In this inspiration, I'd like to share a story about how two different leaders reacted to the same stressful situation.

A few years back, I was working at one of the big four Australian banks. During that period, our division was facing a challenging time. The two primary leaders of our division were under immense pressure and stress, having to deal with dissatisfied and occasionally intimidating stakeholders.

The responses of these two leaders to this stressful situation were markedly different. One leader reacted with frustration and anger. I remember her coming out of difficult meetings with a grim expression, dropping her notepad onto her desk with an audible sigh. Her behaviour often made me feel uneasy and added to my stress.

In contrast, the other leader responded with a sense of playfulness. Despite experiencing the same level of stress, she would defuse tense situations with humour. I distinctly remember she would even sometimes almost be skipping like a little girl. This behaviour, clearly not typical in serious office environments, was her defensive reaction to the stressful situation. Not only did I feel safer around her, but her cheerful disposition also brightened my day.

This experience served as an insightful case study for me, demonstrating how a senior leader's attitude can impact their teams. The leader with a playful mood, managed to absorb the stress and shield her team, while the frustrated leader passed the stress down to her team.

Research has shown that our brains have an emotional circuitry for play, which is linked to exploration and dopamine release (yes, play is fun!). This circuitry fosters brain plasticity, leading to better learning, innovation, and creativity when activated.

There can sometimes be a disconnect between what a person values and what they are required to do at work. Exceptional leaders strive to foster a playful work environment. This playfulness not only encourages innovation and creativity but also serves as a buffer against stress during challenging times.

Playfulness, Personal life & Professional life

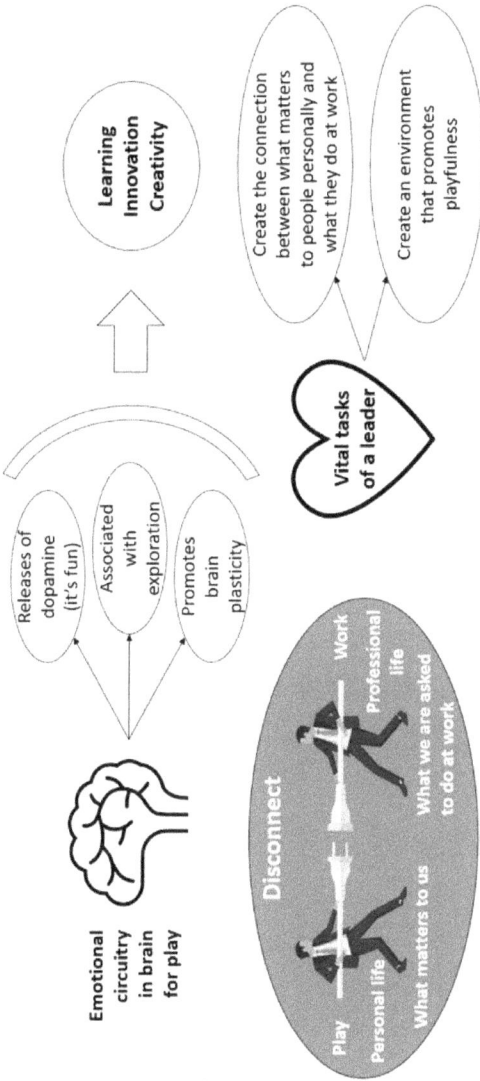

Emotional circuitry in brain for play

Releases of dopamine (it's fun)

Associated with exploration

Promotes brain plasticity

Learning
Innovation
Creativity

Vital tasks of a leader

Create the connection between what matters to people personally and what they do at work

Create an environment that promotes playfulness

Disconnect

Play
Personal life
What matters to us

Work
Professional life
What we are asked to do at work

BASED ON RESEARCH BY DANIEL GOLEMAN & DANIEL SIEGEL

| 37 |

Inspiration 37: The Leader, The Expert, and The Politician!

Being a boss is not necessarily equal to being a leader. According to Simon Sinek,[17] true leaders are those who take care of their people and, in difficult times, choose to put others' needs ahead of their own. In Sinek's view, leadership is a choice, not a rank or position.

Effective leaders possess certain skills that enable them to foster an environment where their teams can thrive. These leadership skills, which include the 12 emotional intelligence competencies discussed in previous inspirations, empower the leader to inspire a vision for their teams and create an environment where everyone can be at their best. To illustrate this concept of leadership, I have made three profiles for bosses in organisations: the Leader, the Expert, and the Politician.

Persona A ("The Leader")

This person excels at leadership skills and chooses to be a leader. She's a great listener, cares for people, and has considerable emotional intelligence. She also chooses to put others' needs ahead of her own, creating an environment where her team can be at their best. Over time, her leadership qualities lead to more senior positions as she is promoted to higher positions of authority. She's a lifelong learner and through it all, she keeps polishing her leadership skills, getting better every day.

Persona B ("The Expert")

This person is highly skilled at their craft. She might be an incredible salesperson, a superstar computer programmer, or a wizard at marketing. Because she is doing such a great job and achieving outstanding results, she gets promoted. Now, instead of being accountable for the outcome of her own work, she is accountable for the outcome of others.

Suddenly she needs a completely different skillset. If she was great at selling, it doesn't mean she'll be great at leading a sales team. If she was a brilliant programmer, it doesn't mean she can inspire a team of programmers. And if she was a successful marketer, it doesn't mean she can take care of a team of marketing professionals.

In short, she now needs leadership skills that she may or may not have. If she's willing to learn them and chooses to put the needs of others in front of her own, she will become a true leader. Otherwise, she will just remain a boss.

Persona C ("The Politician")

This person is highly ambitious, wants to reach the top, and will do whatever it takes to get there. She is super smart and, with diligence, can bend an environment to her will. She manipulates people in a subtle way and, using Machiavellian tactics, climbs the corporate ladder.

She is probably gifted with both emotional intelligence competencies and leadership skills but chooses not to put the needs of others in front of her own. Many people don't trust her, but they can't do anything about it because she's too powerful.

* * *

Please note that the above profiles are generalised archetypes to facilitate understanding. Reality is much more complex, and it's not possible to categorise an individual into a single box. Most people exhibit a mix of these profiles.

| 38 |

Inspiration 38: The Wise Enterprise!

In one of the previous inspirations, we explored the concept of "Doing what's right, not what's easy". But how can one discern what is right?

Sometimes, it's clear what's right and what's wrong, e.g., we don't want to break the law, we don't want to be dishonest, and we want to serve our customers' best interests.

But sometimes, it's not so easy to figure out what the right thing to do is. E.g., what is the best solution to a problem? What is the most effective way of delivering an outcome? How should we manage conflicting priorities?

In order to answer these challenging questions, we need to become wiser. Philosopher Valerie Tiberius defines wisdom as the set of dispositions, skills, and policies that help us deliberate about what matters in life and then translating that into choices and actions. It is basically figuring out what is good and then achieving those things while helping others to do so as well.

I believe there are four capabilities that can help us make wiser decisions in organisations. These capabilities are:

- Systems Thinking
- Emotional Intelligence
- Leadership
- Organisation Transformation

I explore this topic in depth in my book, "The Wise Enterprise: Reshaping Your Organisation for the Age of Uncertainty".[18] For a concise overview of this concept, you can listen to my interview with David Frizzell[19] on his famous podcast, Team Guru.

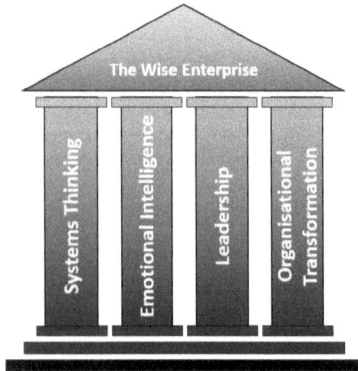

| 39 |

Inspiration 39: The Blind Men and the Elephant

Rumi, the 13th-century Persian philosopher and mystic, shared in his book Masnavi, an insightful ancient Indian parable about a group of people trying to identify a mysterious object in a dark room. This object, of course, is an elephant, but the people don't know that. The room is too dark; they can't see anything.

One person picks up the trunk of the elephant, examines it with his hand, and then shouts out, "It's a large hose". Another person touches the ear of the elephant and says, "No, you idiot. It's a large leather fan". The next person is touching the legs of the elephant and says, "You are both wrong. This object is a tree". And so on. Each person was touching one part of the elephant and describing only that part.

Rumi goes on to say that if these people had a candle in their hand, all their disagreements would disappear. We need to stop sensing reality with just our hands; we need to use all our senses.

When we make decisions at work, our perception of "the system" is like the sense of touch in a dark room. But we need to see the whole system in its entirety. So, where can we find a candle? **How can we *understand* the whole system?**

Deep insight can only be attained by "going to the work." This takes the Lean concept of Gemba a step further. In Lean manufacturing, Gemba is when managers spend time working from the factory floor where the actual work is happening. But what we mean by "going to the work" is following a unit of work from its initiation to completion, observing its journey as it is handled by multiple individuals and handed off within the organisation's silos. The person 'going to the work' will spend time observing and, if possible, performing some of the steps within the entire value stream (process).

Having theoretical discussions and deliberating concepts in a meeting room is like touching the elephant in the dark. To understand what is really going on, we need to "go to the work" and experience it first-hand.

Activities like listening to client calls, double jacking, value stream mapping, and sitting and working with other teams are great examples of how to start "going to the work" to understand the system first-hand.

| 40 |

Inspiration 40: The Φ-losophy of Success!

In this inspiration, we delve into a technical yet intriguing subject—cybernetics. Cybernetics is a scientific field that studies control and communication in both living and nonliving systems. The term 'Cybernetics' originates from the Greek word 'Kubernetes', meaning 'He who steers'.

When we view an organisation through the lens of Cybernetics, it behaves much like an organism within an ecosystem. It grows, protects itself, interacts with its surroundings, and adapts its behaviour in response to external challenges.

In Cybernetics, an organism's capacity to handle new challenges is represented by a measure called "integrated information", denoted by the Greek letter Φ (phi). This measure is related to the system's ability to process information and respond to new situations it hasn't previously encountered. Therefore, a higher Φ level generally indicates more success in devising novel solutions when confronting new challenges.

So, how do you calculate Φ? While the exact calculation can get a bit technical, in simple terms, Φ is correlated with the diversity of thought within the system and the number of connections between the system's agents. These 'agents' could be neurons in a brain if we are talking about an organism, or employees if we are talking about an organisation. By encouraging a diversity of thought and creating more connections among people in an organisation, we can increase its Φ, or 'resilience and adaptability score'.

These are some ways that you can boost your company's Φ and make it more successful:

- Network with new people and forge friendships across the company.
- Collaborate closely with colleagues you haven't worked with before.
- Regularly visit the office and spend time catching up with colleagues in person.
- Encourage thoughtful disagreement.
- Seek diverse perspectives.
- Request feedback from colleagues you don't usually work closely with.
- Reach out to someone whose job you believe is unaffected by your work, and explore how your work might impact theirs.
- Most importantly, set aside dedicated time to expand your relationships and diversity of thought.

If you wish to explore this concept further, I've extensively discussed it on a podcast episode with the renowned author Bobby Azarian[20].

Integrated information of an organisation – from the cybernetics theory

$$\Phi \propto D \times n$$

D : Diversity of thought

n : Number of relationships

Capability of a system to succeed in its environment is co-related with the diversity of thought within the system and the number of relationships between the agents in the system

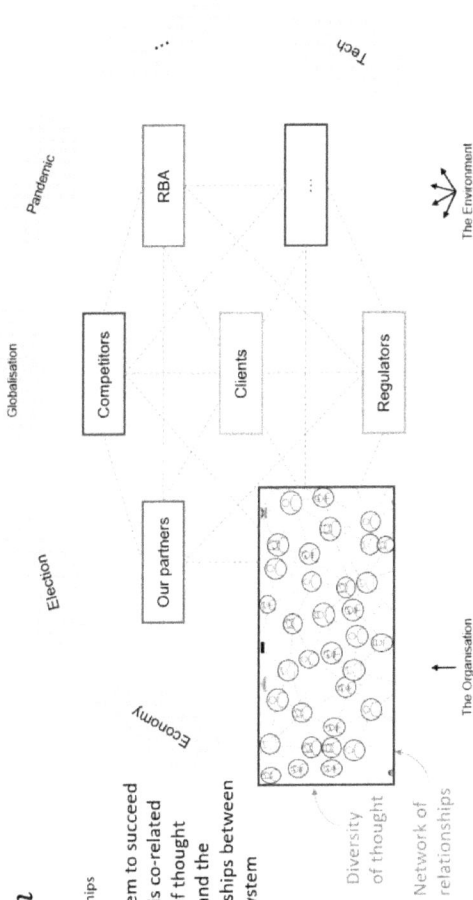

Economy

Election

Globalisation

Pandemic

Tech

...

Our partners

Competitors

Clients

Regulators

RBA

...

The Environment

The Organisation

Diversity of thought

Network of relationships

| 41 |

Inspiration 41: Elevate the Game!

> "We cannot solve our problems with the same thinking we used when we created them." ~ Albert Einstein

Often, paradigm-shifting innovative ideas originate from outsiders, not experts within a field. This is because it's typically easier for outsiders to think outside the box and challenge prevailing work methods. But how can we foster an environment that encourages everyone to think outside the box?

In one of his engaging lectures, renowned American organisational theorist and Systems Thinker Professor Russell Ackoff shared a story about creative problem-solving and outside-the-box thinking. This story was about an old office building in New York struggling with long queues for their elevators.

To address this issue, the building management hired a consulting firm that was an expert in this area. The consultants charged a substantial fee and proposed several solutions: adding more elevators, installing faster elevators, or implementing computerised elevators that take the most optimal path.

The building management soon realised that, given the age of the building, none of these options were financially viable or technologically feasible. The only remaining solution was to demolish the building and construct a new high-rise.

In a desperate move, the management team organised an ideation workshop, including some junior employees. The workshop aimed to generate creative solutions to this problem, with the rules being that no idea was too crazy, and no one was allowed to criticise anyone's idea, regardless of its eccentricity. The only comment you were allowed to give on anyone's idea was, "If you think it's not going to work, you could only suggest how to make it work".

Despite numerous ideas being discussed in the workshop, they were still stuck. One of the junior team members, who had been quiet the entire time and hadn't contributed any ideas, was asked for his thoughts. The junior team member hesitated, saying, "I have an idea, but I don't want to share it because people might say it's not going to work, and I don't want to look stupid in front of everyone!"

Everyone assured him they would not dismiss his idea and would try to understand his thought process. The young man then said, "We are trying to solve the wrong problem here. The problem is not that people are waiting; the problem is that people are bored! So, we need to find a way to entertain them while they wait."

After further exploring this idea and conducting various experiments, such as installing mirrors and altering the elevator lobby's architecture, the company managed to solve the problem and save the building.

The moral of this story is that to encourage out-of-the-box thinking, we need to welcome unconventional ideas. Most unconventional ideas may initially seem impractical or even irrelevant, and people may feel vulnerable when they put them forward. Therefore, we must be patient and gentle. Then, we can ask ourselves: 'Is there any way we can make this idea work in our context?' Generating creative ideas in organisations is akin to composing a new melody or painting a new masterpiece. The artist needs to slow down, connect to their senses, feel safe, and be inspired to generate creative ideas.

When we are under delivery pressure and working through tasks, we are usually in a different state of mind – we are thinking inside the box. To think outside the box, we need to slow down and enter an artistic, creative state of mind.

| 42 |

Inspiration 42: 42!

In his brilliant book, "The Hitchhiker's Guide to the Galaxy," Douglas Adams tells us a funny story about a race of hyper-intelligent aliens who build a supercomputer named Deep Thought to find the answer to the ultimate question: What is the answer to life, the universe, and everything?

After 7.5 million years, Deep Thought announces that it has found the answer. A grand celebration ensues, and many beings from across the galaxy join to hear the answer. However, in an anticlimactic moment, Deep Thought announces that the answer to life, the universe, and everything is 42. Seeing the disappointment in the crowd, Deep Thought states that the question itself was poorly constructed. What does it even mean, the answer to life, the universe, and everything?

The aliens then ask the computer what the ultimate question is. But Deep Thought states it is not powerful enough to calculate the ultimate question. To do that, an even more powerful computer needs to be created. This new computer being constructed is the planet Earth, with all its inhabitants.

This story prompts us to consider the ultimate question in leadership. As discussed in previous inspirations, it is not always the responsibility of a leader to provide solutions or answers. Often, effective leaders guide individuals to discover the appropriate answer within their own context. So, what is the ultimate question a leader can ask?

David Marquet, the author of "Turn the Ship Around," suggests two great questions a leader could ask: "What are we trying to achieve?" and "What does success look like to you?"

These two questions are examples of Socratic questioning, a method employed by the renowned Greek philosopher Socrates. Such questions are driven by a sense of curiosity and a desire to explore ideas on a deeper level. Here are more examples of Socratic questions:

- What do you mean by this?
- What is the main point you are trying to make?
- What is the problem we are trying to solve?
- Could you put this another way?
- What are your assumptions?
- Could you give me an example?
- What evidence are you basing this on?
- How can you find out if this is true?
- What is the counterargument to that?
- What are the implications of that?
- What if you are wrong?
- What would it be like if …?

- Why is that important to you?

Here are some rules of thumb for asking powerful questions:

- Avoid yes/no questions such as "Do you think ..." as these limit the boundaries of thought.
- Refrain from asking 'why' questions as they can be perceived as intimidating. Instead, ask "What are some reasons for ..." The only acceptable 'why' question is "Why is this important to you?"
- 'What' questions are generally the most effective.

| 43 |

Inspiration 43: The Subtle Art of Not Doing!

The 10th principle of the "Agile Manifesto" states, "Simplicity –the art of maximising the amount of work not done–is essential!" This principle has sparked much debate. What does "maximising work not done" mean? Isn't this contrary to our goals? Shouldn't we strive to accomplish more work rather than less?

Complexity increases when the number of interacting variables increases. By increasing the number of processes, systems, and solutions in an organisation, we inadvertently increase the number of interacting variables, thereby making things more complex.

When we are faced with problems, we often jump into solution mode, devising a new process or implementing a new technological solution. Over time, the accumulation of these processes and solutions can lead to layers of complexity in our environment. Instead of immediately resorting to solution mode, we should return to the drawing board, looking at the big picture to eliminate the root cause of the problem.

This does not mean that we have to avoid new processes or technology solutions. Rather, when devising solutions, we should question whether there's a simpler way to achieve the same outcomes. In essence, how can we accomplish more with less? How can we work smarter instead of harder?

The Boy Scouts of America[21] have a simple rule: "Leave the campground cleaner than you found it." This powerful rule prompts us to consider whether our solutions make the environment more complex and messy or make it simpler and cleaner. How are we leaving the campground for those who follow us?

Crafting simple solutions isn't easy. According to Steve Jobs, "It takes a lot of hard work, to make something simple, to truly understand the underlying challenges and come up with elegant solutions." This sentiment was echoed in Apple's first marketing brochure in 1977, which declared, "Simplicity is the ultimate sophistication."

To create simple and elegant solutions, we have to absorb the complexity. It requires considerable effort and out-of-the-box thinking to ensure our solutions are simple and elegant. This concept is encapsulated in the following quote:

> "If I had more time, I would have written you a shorter letter"
> ~ attributed to Blaise Pascal.

Typical Apple Product

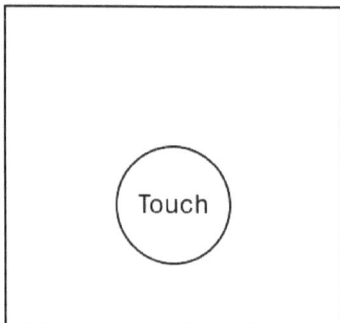

Touch

A Google Product

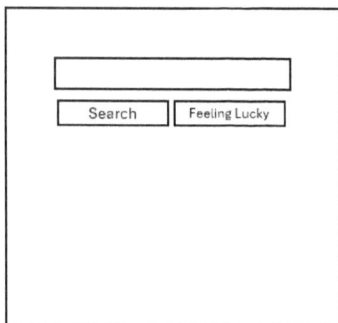

| Search | Feeling Lucky |

Your Company's Product

First Name [   ]   Type [   ]   CNG
                                                  A-42
Last Name [   ]   AGT Status [ ][ ][ ]   APG?
                                                  MT-S
SSN [   ] FT [ ]   Version # [   ] PT [ ] NEW
                                                  NEW 2
Phone 1 [ ][ ][   ]   HCT ID [   ] NEW 3
Phone 2 [ ][ ][   ]   Priority ○A+ ●A   ○ B   ADD
                                                  DEL
Address 1 [   ]   Address 2 [   ]

[Apply] [OK] [Save] [Cancel] [Undo] [Redo] [Help] [Errors]

INSPIRED BY ERIC BOURKE

| 44 |

Inspiration 44: The Devolution of Excellence!

Imagine walking into a room filled with antique furniture. Each piece tells a story of craftsmanship that has withstood the test of time. A few years ago, while searching for high-quality and nicely designed furniture for our home, my wife and I stumbled upon the world of antiques.

The durability, quality, and beauty of the antiques were not even comparable to what you could get today, even at the most expensive furniture shops. Take, for example, our 150-year-old table, which is still in better shape today than the table we bought less than ten years ago.

This makes you wonder: Why don't they make them like they used to? Why is everything today ugly and low quality? There are many reasons for that, but one of the culprits is the concept of division of labour.

In the 17th century, before the Industrial Revolution, if you needed a table, you would approach a master carpenter. This artisan, with years of training and experience, would create a custom-made piece for you. The process was slow, but the result was a product of superior quality and design, a product the artisan took pride in.

To work in a carpenter's shop an apprentice had to spend years perfecting his craft and become highly skilled. The person in charge of production typically performed most of the work from start to finish. They had a vision for the whole product and were capable of executing most of the steps in the process on their own.

However, the advent of the Industrial Revolution brought significant changes. The invention of various powered machines and standardisation led to increased production volumes and decreased unit costs. One of the key concepts that enabled this was the concept of division of labour.

Adam Smith, in his renowned book "The Wealth of Nations," illustrates the profound impact of division of labour on pin manufacturing. He demonstrated that with the right division of labour, ten workers could produce thousands of pins each day. Conversely, a single person attempting to do all the work might struggle to produce even one pin per day.

This shift in labour practices transformed the workforce. Work became simple and repetitive. Workers no longer needed to understand the product they were producing. They became cogs in a machine; a sentiment echoed in this shocking quote from 19th-century management consultant Frederick Taylor: "One of the very first requirements for a man who is fit to handle pig iron as a regular occupation is that he shall be so stupid and so phlegmatic that he more nearly resembles in his mental make-up the ox than any other type. The man who is mentally alert and intelligent is for this very reason entirely unsuited to what would, for him, be the grinding monotony of work of this character. Therefore the workman who is best suited to handling pig iron is unable to understand the real science of doing this class of work."

Proponents of this approach, like Frederick Taylor, would argue that someone operating simple machinery in a factory doesn't need to have a holistic understanding of the product. They don't need to be creative, and their pride in their work is irrelevant. All that's required is their hands and their compliance; they can leave their brains at the door when they enter the factory.

This approach to management was incredibly successful, leading industrialists to apply it universally throughout the 19th and 20th centuries. However, the landscape is very different today. Our world is complex, and products are no longer sold in isolation. They are part of an intertwined web of products and services. The division of labour, while efficient for simple tasks, falls short when it comes to complex products and services.

Work is now highly skilled again. A software engineer writing code for a car's seat adjustment function, for example, is capable enough to understand how the car seat is made. In fact, to produce high-quality software, the software engineer must see the big picture. They need to have domain knowledge and understand the whole product they are producing.

Today, we're seeing a shift in organisational structures again. Many are moving away from siloed structures with strict division of labour to more collaborative and transparent structures. Today's most successful organisations are organised in cross-functional teams that are collectively responsible for delivering customer outcomes. Workers are encouraged to cross-skill and develop an understanding of the whole process. This shift towards a holistic understanding of outcomes allows today's employees to take pride in their work, reminiscent of the pre-Industrial Revolution era when artisans took pride in their craftsmanship. As W. Edwards Deming, a renowned engineer, statistician, professor, author, and management consultant, once eloquently put it:

> "All anyone asks for is a chance to work with pride."

Inspiration 45: The Data Delusion!

One of the buzzwords permeating the business world in recent years is data-informed decision-making. Decisions informed by data are often seen as more reliable than those based on expert experience or intuition. Moreover, data-informed decisions offer a more robust justification for the reasoning that led to the decision. The importance of data and measurements in management and business administration has always been recognised, as evidenced by the famous quote from renowned management consultant Peter Drucker: "You can't manage what you don't measure."

While I agree that data and measurements are critical inputs for business decision-making, I believe incorrect use of data can be dangerous or even catastrophic. There are several key points to consider when making data-informed decisions:

1. Sample size matters:

To use data correctly, a rudimentary understanding of statistics is necessary. To have a reasonable confidence level and margin of error, data must be collected from a minimum sample size. Basing decisions on small sample sizes is risky, as it may result in biases, false positives, or completely off-track conclusions. The data points you've gathered might merely be exceptions rather than the norm.

Calculating sample size involves complex mathematical operations, but numerous online calculators are available. Simply input your population size, desired confidence level, and acceptable margin of error to determine the required minimum sample size.

$$\text{Sample size} = \frac{\dfrac{z^2 \times p\,(1-p)}{e^2}}{1 + \left(\dfrac{z^2 \times p\,(1-p)}{e^2 N}\right)}$$

If accessing a large enough sample size for your decision-making is not feasible, it may be better to consider qualitative factors, experience, or even your gut feeling. The danger with small sample sizes is not only the potential for inaccurate data but also the illusion of a scientific approach, believing decisions are based on solid data and evidence while they are not.

2. There Are Lies, Damned Lies, and Statistics

Mark Twain was among the first to use the phrase "Lies, damned lies, and statistics" to highlight the dangers of misusing data to manipulate opinions and influence decision-making. Data can be cherry-picked and interpreted in ways that support a particular viewpoint. It's crucial to maintain an objective and scientific approach when collecting data. Consider what your hypothesis is, what needs to be measured to validate it, and how it can be falsified.

For instance, I once facilitated a workshop for a client grappling with a high turnover rate of key talent. An HR team representative claimed they were sure people were leaving due to the lack of a career progression program, as exit questionnaire data confirmed this. However, a perceptive individual pointed out that employees might be providing this reason because the surveys did not offer options for the actual reasons for their departure. The questionnaires have been effectively leading the employees to give a particular answer, rather than truthful ones.

3. The act of measurement changes what is being measured

The famous uncertainty principle in quantum mechanics points out that the act of measurement influences the system being measured. This principle is also relevant in the business world, where measurement can impact people's behaviour.

These behavioural changes can be desirable but may also lead to negative, unforeseen consequences. For example, measuring call handling time in a call centre will likely affect team members' behaviour, prompting them to conclude calls more quickly. While reducing call time may seem beneficial initially, it can lead to unintended outcomes. Complex cases requiring more effort might be deprioritised or avoided. Customer representatives might be incentivised to dismiss callers hastily, advising them to seek help online or use the chat system instead. And ironically, those customers whose problems have not been solved when they called first, may call again, resulting in longer call queues.

| 46 |

Inspiration 46: The Unseen Advisor!

"There is a voice that doesn't use words, listen." ~ Rumi, 13th-century Persian philosopher and mystic.

What is the voice Rumi is referring to in this verse? It's our inner voice, our intuition.

Contrary to the belief that business decision-making should be based solely on hard data and rigorous analysis, intuition can also play a significant role. A study cited by the renowned American author Daniel Goleman[22] reveals that successful entrepreneurs in California rely on a blend of data and their gut feelings when making decisions. These entrepreneurs are voracious gatherers of data; they delve deep into the numbers and scrutinise every detail. Yet, they also listen to their gut feelings, checking their final decisions against this internal barometer.

But what exactly is this 'gut feeling'? It is connected to a primitive part of the brain known as the *insula*, which is neurologically linked to your gut. The insula compiles your experiences and knowledge, and processes information cues that might be invisible to your conscious mind.

In the famous "Iowa Gambling Task" study by Antonio Damasio[23], participants were asked to choose cards from four decks, with some decks being rigged to lose more often. The study found that it took the participants about 80 cards to consciously understand the decks were rigged, but it only took them about 50 cards to start expressing a hunch about which deck was bad. But what is incredible is that only after about 10 cards, their bodies began physically responding as they were reaching for the bad decks.

The participants were connected to a machine that measured their galvanic skin response (increased sweatiness), which revealed that healthy participants showed a "stress" reaction to hovering over the bad decks only after 10 trials. This is a remarkable finding considering it took 80 trials to figure it out consciously.

Now, the question arises: how can we access this vast reservoir of information available through our gut feelings more effectively? How can we better connect with our intuition? The answer lies in cultivating body awareness, mindfulness, and self-awareness. With practice, we can learn to become more attuned to our bodies. By becoming aware of how emotions manifest in physiological responses, we can tap into this significant source of information.

One excellent body awareness exercise is observing how your emotions physiologically manifest in your body. For instance, the next time you feel stressed, start paying attention to what is happening in your body.

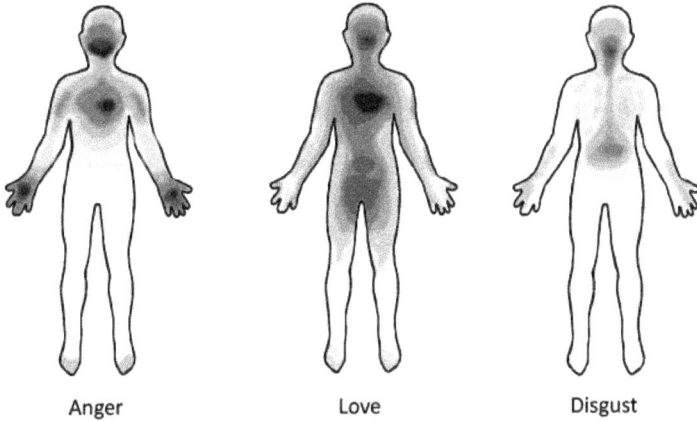

| Anger | Love | Disgust |

Body maps of emotions

Nevertheless, we must exercise caution when utilising our intuition. I believe there are two distinct types of intuition:

Type 1:

This type involves the ability to pick up on subtle information cues that may not be accessible to us consciously. An example of this is the rigged card scenario mentioned earlier. It could also apply to situations where all evidence suggests that a project will be delivered successfully, but your intuition, informed by years of experience as a project manager, indicates a potential failure.

Type 2:

This type of intuition relates to precognitions and psychic activities. It includes instances such as waking up with a premonition about a friend you haven't seen in a year or knowing specifics about events across time and space. This form of intuition is dangerous and should be avoided. Pursuing this type of intuition carries the risk of emotional imbalance, obsession, and mental and psychological disorders.

As someone who values spirituality, I believe accessing spiritual information channels should be reserved for personal enlightenment. Utilising these channels to acquire powers or achieve success in this world is unethical and dangerous.

Inspiration 47: Why 70% of Transformations Fail!

According to McKinsey & Co, 70% of transformation programs fail[24]. Despite this, nearly every organisation today is engaged in some form of transformation. For these efforts to be successful, they must be agile, empirically driven, and user-centric. Here are three primary reasons why many transformation initiatives stumble:

1. Not having enough focus on User Experience:

Often, the very individuals who will use the new systems—the internal customers—are not given due consideration. Whether it's adapting ways of working or undergoing a digital transformation, their active participation is crucial. The most successful transformations involve these users throughout the process, allowing them to contribute to the design of the new system of work.

Organisations often adopt a top-down approach, designing the future state behind closed doors and then rolling it out across the organisation. This method fails to include those who are ultimately affected by the changes, depriving the design process of critical user input. The rationale behind this approach is usually the fear that too many voices can stall progress. While this fear is justified, there are proven methods to manage this risk. These methods facilitate co-creation and ensure a robust framework is in place to avoid getting tangled in endless debates.

2. Assumption of Perfect Knowledge:

Organisations often design the end state upfront and then implement it without empirically validating their design. Things in reality are often very different from things on paper. Organisations are living systems, and we can never be entirely confident how they will react to the changes being rolled out.

Transformation programs typically encompass numerous interacting components and a high degree of complexity. Our target state design is based on many assumptions that need to be empirically validated as the changes are being rolled out. We cannot afford to wait until the end of the transformation initiative to test if it has achieved the desired outcomes. By that time, it would be too late, as all the time and budget would have been expended.

3. Using a 'Big Bang' Approach instead of an incremental agile delivery:

Many transformation initiatives span 1 to 3 years. During this period, the world does not stand still; numerous factors such as regulations, customer expectations, technology, market conditions, the global competitive landscape, the economy, key leadership personnel, and the strategic direction of the organisation may change. We must be able to respond to these changes as they occur.

This is particularly tragic in agile transformation programs. Agile ways of working are founded on customer-centricity, empirical verification, and iterative development. Yet, most agile transformations ironically adopt a waterfall approach. They spend months or even years designing the end state, followed by developing a roadmap for the implementation, and then managing the rollout according to this predefined roadmap.

The Solution - The Model Office Approach:

A proven strategy for transformation is the 'model office' approach. This method starts by selecting a small, cross-functional team of 6 to 9 people who are taken out of their day jobs. Their new role is to devise a new system of work. It's essential that this group is cross-functional, representing various divisions of the company, to bring diversity of thought and perspective and to break down silos within the organisation.

This 'model office' team is tasked with experimenting with new approaches, and they have an experienced coach to guide them through the process and challenge them. They will spend

6 to 8 weeks studying the current system of work and then develop creative and drastically different methods for conducting business. As the model office is small and the risk is well contained, they have support from leadership to come up with creative and unconventional approaches.

The team has a licence to do anything they want as long as they don't break the law. They operate in parallel with the broader business, and work intake will be load-balanced—a small percentage of the work goes to the model office, while the majority goes to the broader business.

After the model office has demonstrated that their new way of working is effective, typically within 3 to 6 months, the scaling process begins. But to scale, we will not roll out the new system of work to the rest of the business. Instead, we will roll people into the model office. Every month, a new group goes through the same process of forming a cross-functional team, studying the system, and then integrating with the model office.

As new cohorts join, any issues with scaling are addressed. What works for a team of 6 may not work for a team of 600. This incremental integration ensures that as the team grows, the ways of working are refined and validated for larger groups.

This model office approach keeps the transformation risk contained and manageable. There are two concurrent operational groups: one using the new way of working, and the other using the old, familiar, and proven method. As the model office expands, the group using the old system diminishes.

In contrast to the waterfall approach to transformation, where initial analysis and roadmap construction may give an illusion of control, the model office approach offers a tangible measure of progress and success. The waterfall approach may alleviate our fear, but the risk will still be there, hiding under piles of documentation and sign-offs. While KPIs may show green and roadmaps may indicate great progress, we still end up with a situation where 70% of transformation programs fail to deliver what they set out to achieve.

For an in-depth discussion on this approach, you may refer to the interview I conducted at the EI Evolution Summit in 2022[25]

4 EASY WAYS TO TRANSFORM YOUR ORGANISATION

Translate
$$\begin{bmatrix} 1 & 0 & X \\ 0 & 1 & Y \\ 0 & 0 & 1 \end{bmatrix}$$

Rotate about origin
$$\begin{bmatrix} \cos\theta & \sin\theta & 0 \\ -\sin\theta & \cos\theta & 0 \\ 0 & 0 & 1 \end{bmatrix}$$

Reflect about x-axis
$$\begin{bmatrix} 1 & 0 & 0 \\ 0 & -1 & 0 \\ 0 & 0 & 1 \end{bmatrix}$$

Scale about origin
$$\begin{bmatrix} W & 0 & 0 \\ 0 & H & 0 \\ 0 & 0 & 1 \end{bmatrix}$$

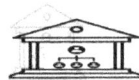

| 48 |

Inspiration 48: When Waterfall is Better Than Agile!

As an enterprise agile coach and a management consultant, I dedicate my workdays to guiding organisations in transitioning from a waterfall delivery approach to a more dynamic, agile, incremental delivery approach. But there are certain situations where waterfall actually works better than agile:

1. When building large physical structures:

The Waterfall approach to delivery has been used for thousands of years in construction projects. The process of building large physical structures is inherently sequential.

Having an agile mindset of experimentation and early verification is always helpful, even when building physical things.

However, we cannot escape the sequential nature of construction project delivery: requirements first, then analysis, design, development, and final verification. If technological advancements, such as 3D printing, enable cheap and quick prototyping of quality construction materials, we might see agile used in construction projects in the future.

2. Low-risk projects:

For projects with minimal risk—those that are straightforward and have been executed repeatedly—Waterfall can be more suitable. For example, suppose you're building a low-cost WordPress website from a predefined template, and you know exactly what needs to be done and have done it many times before. In that case, there's no need for experimentation and incremental delivery.

3. When your risk is so high that if you get it wrong, people will die:

For example, certain types of medical software are used in organ transplants to help identify the chances of rejection or acceptance of the organ by the recipient's body. The level of precision and rigour required for these types of projects makes it harder to experiment with MVPs and incremental delivery.

4. *When you have no choice:*

Sometimes, especially in government or defence projects, you are constrained by the environment. When multiple contractors work on different components of a larger system, like an airplane or a tank, and the requirements are set by the government, it's not always feasible to adopt an end-to-end agile process. Here, you do the best you can within the constraints.

| 49 |

Inspiration 49: Elastic Fantastic!

Adaptability is defined as one's ability to adjust to new conditions. Adaptability can manifest itself in different ways. On short timescales, an adaptable person can do context-switching quickly and easily. On long timescales, an adaptable person can change their strategic plans quickly and respond to changing conditions. Research suggests that among all social and emotional competencies, adaptability is the strongest predictor of career success, career satisfaction, and life satisfaction.[26]

There are various strategies that can help us become more adaptable. In this inspiration, I'll introduce two strategies that could help increase your adaptability.

1. Mindset shift from focusing on output to outcome

Let's do a thought experiment together. Let's imagine you want to swim across a river. You look across the river and pick the location in a straight line on the other side of the river. Your plan is to go there because this is the shortest path. As you start swimming, the current of the river is going to take you with it. It would be impossible to reach the original location that you had in mind as you cannot swim faster than the river current. If you try too hard, you'll get tired or may panic and drown.

The only option is to keep swimming forward, accepting that you will not be able to reach your original target across the river. You will eventually end up across the river, but it will be a different location. And that will be fine because your ultimate goal, the outcome you were after, was crossing the river. Similarly, an adaptable person focuses on the outcome they are after and will be flexible with their outputs. The outputs are "a means to an end". If we remain focused on the "means" it will be difficult to be adaptable.

The outcome is our "why", and the output is our "what". The goals we set are typically arbitrary outputs we put in place to achieve our "why". We come up with these goals based on our best knowledge and the conditions as we experience them at the time of goal setting. Those conditions will most likely change as time passes, and we will gain more knowledge as we move along, so those goals need to be updated quickly to enable us to achieve our "why". If we don't do this and fixate on the goals and outputs, we may lose sight of our "why".

No doubt, outputs and goals are needed for planning purposes and to think about what we need to deliver to produce the outcomes. But we must be prepared to let them go quickly as things change and come up with new outputs that will serve us best in our new conditions.

2. Reducing stress and doing more aerobic exercises

The hippocampus is a part of our brains that (among other things) plays an important role in making us adaptable.[27] The neurons in the hippocampus are very sensitive to cortisol (the stress hormone). When we are under prolonged stress, the function of the hippocampus is disrupted, and our adaptability is reduced. In today's fast-paced, technology-dependent world, most people are under elevated cortisol levels throughout the day. So, reducing your stress levels is one of the most effective ways of increasing your adaptability.

Some highly effective strategies to reduce stress are taking a walk in nature, petting an animal, playing with children, extending kindness and compassion, and certain types of meditation.

Another highly effective activity is engaging in aerobic exercises. Aerobic exercises are believed to promote neurogenesis (formation of new brain cells), particularly in the hippocampus area. This, in turn, promotes more plasticity and flexibility in our brains. Neurogenesis could heal potential damage caused by elevated levels of stress in the hippocampus. And it will likely result in our brains becoming more flexible in general, making us more open and adaptable.

Some examples of aerobic exercises include running, swimming, walking, dancing, and most other cardio workouts.

If you're interested in learning more strategies for becoming agile, adaptable, and wise, please check out my best-selling book, "The Wise Enterprise: Reshape Your Organisation for the Age of Uncertainty".

Adaptability is the strongest predictor of career success, career satisfaction, and life satisfaction

Focus on outcome instead of output

Work towards your "why" but change your "what" frequently

More aerobic exercises

running, swimming, walking, dancing, etc. → Neurogenesis in hippocampus → plasticity & flexibility

Reduce Stress

Cortisol ↑

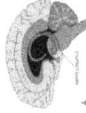

Taking a walk in the nature, petting an animal, playing with children, extending kindness and compassion

| 50 |

Inspiration 50: Flawed Logic and Twisted Truths!

Have you ever been in a meeting where your argument was twisted and used against you? Or perhaps you've experienced a situation where someone managed to sway the group's opinion against your ideas using illogical arguments that didn't even make sense. If so, you might have been a victim of sophistry – the expert use of logical fallacies.

A fallacy is the use of invalid or otherwise flawed reasoning when constructing an argument. We often use fallacies without realising it, as they can appear well-reasoned to the untrained observer and may go unnoticed. To keep conversations on track and prevent them from going in circles, it is crucial to learn to identify fallacies. This allows us to avoid using them in our arguments and, more importantly, to recognise them when used by others and steer the conversation back on course.

While there are over a hundred logical fallacies, I want to discuss five common ones that frequently appear in our conversations:

1. Appeal to Authority:

This fallacy occurs when an argument is deemed true solely because of the authority of the person asserting it, rather than the actual reasoning behind it.

2. Straw Man:

This is one of the most common fallacies and one of the hardest to detect. Typically, the person using this fallacy refutes an argument slightly different from the one actually under discussion without recognising or acknowledging the distinction.

3. Ad Hominem:

This fallacy occurs when the focus of the argument is shifted from the issue at hand to the personal characteristics or credibility of the person making the argument. Instead of addressing the argument itself, the opponent is personally attacked.

4. Circular Reasoning:

Here, the reasoner begins with what they are trying to end up with, often by playing with words.

5. Slippery Slope:

This one is asserting that a proposed, relatively small, first action will inevitably lead to a chain of related events resulting in a significant and negative event.

Let's consider a few examples. Suppose a solutions architect has made a design decision that you must use dependency injection in a specific module to facilitate easier unit testing. Here's how we might use these fallacies to argue against this decision:

Appeal to Authority:

"I have been writing code for 20 years, and I know it's best not to use dependency injection in this module."

Straw Man:

"You want us to use dependency injection everywhere, which is simply not possible."

Ad Hominem:

"You got the last design decision terribly wrong. I'm not going to trust your decisions anymore."

Circular Reasoning:

"Dependency injection is the worst design pattern ever because dependency injection doesn't work."

Slippery Slope:

"Today you ask us to use dependency injection, and tomorrow you'll ask us to hardcode values to make unit testing easier."

In none of the cases above did we provide a logical reason why dependency injection should not be used. An expert facilitator must be able to identify fallacies when used and gently guide the conversation back on track. For instance, you could ask, "What are the reasons you believe dependency injection should not be used?"

It's important to note that fallacies are often used, consciously or subconsciously, to evoke strong emotions and interfere with our reasoning power. Therefore, it's essential to manage emotions when identifying fallacies. Also, remember that most people are not aware of fallacies, so it's not helpful to call someone out for using one. They probably don't even know what a fallacy is. Instead, simply notice it and gently steer the conversation back on track.

The best way to practise this skill is by first being self-aware and identifying when you are subconsciously using fallacies yourself. This will not only enable you to identify others' fallacies but will also help you build better, bulletproof arguments that cannot be easily torn down.

| 51 |

Inspiration 51: The Mythbuster's Guide to Agility!

Like most buzzwords, "Agile" comes with a lot of baggage. When people hear the term, they bring their own preconceptions, personal experiences, what they have read online, what they have experienced in the organisations, personal challenges, and successes to the table. This is the inherent challenge with buzzwords - we believe we're communicating effectively, but our individual interpretations of these terms can vary significantly. Even though we're using the same words, we mean different things by those words.

If you were to ask ten different organisations to define "Agile," you'd likely receive ten different responses. There are many misconceptions about agile in the industry. So, in this inspiration, we will debunk some of the myths about agile.

The Agile Methodology

First and foremost, Agile is not a methodology, framework, model, or tool—it's the capability to respond to change quickly and easily. Agile is as fluid as water, formless yet powerful enough to cut steel and carve canyons.

You Are Either Agile or Not

Agile is not a binary state; it's not a switch that's either on or off. It's a spectrum of capability, with varying degrees of adaptability and responsiveness to change.

The Pace of Delivery

While some might think Agile is about delivering faster, it's actually about responding to change faster. While it is important to deliver quickly, the primary objective of agile is to empower us to respond to change easily and quickly.

Being a Feature Factory

Agile is not about delivering more features; it's about delivering fewer features—but the right ones. It's the art of ensuring that the features delivered are the ones that truly matter.

Doing Showcases

Agile isn't just showcasing your work every iteration; it's about seeking feedback and learning every iteration. It's a continuous loop of feedback, learning, and improvement.

Best Practices

Following a framework is not the end goal of Agile; rather, it's about continuously evolving and improving your processes. It's about diagnosing what's not working and fixing it, not blindly adhering to a set of rules.

Resource Efficiency

Agile shifts the focus from increasing resource efficiency to increasing flow efficiency. It's about optimising the flow of work, rather than just keeping everyone busy.

Maximising Utilisaiton

Ensuring people are utilised more is not the aim; Agile ensures people have discretionary time for creativity. It's about giving people the space to innovate and create.

Increasing Velocity

In Agile, measuring and increasing velocity takes a backseat to measuring and decreasing lead time. It's about how quickly you can deliver value from start to finish, not just how many story points you deliver.

Perfectionism

Lastly, Agile favours pragmatism over perfectionism. It's about making practical, value-driven decisions within your constraints, not chasing theoretical solutions.

Agile is not	Agile is
A methodology, framework, model, or tool	The capability to respond to change quickly and easily
A binary state	A spectrum of capability
Delivering Faster	Responding to change faster
Delivering more features	Delivering less features
Pumping out features faster	Ensuring the right features are delivered
Showcasing your work every iteration	Seeking feedback and learning every iteration
Following a framework	Evolving and improving your processes continuously
Following scrum rules religiously even when they don't work	Figuring out what is causing Scrum not to work and fixing that
Increasing resource efficiency	Increasing flow efficiency
Ensuring people are utilised more	Ensuring people have discretionary time for creativity
Measuring and increasing velocity	Measuring and decreasing lead time
Perfectionism	Pragmatism

| 52 |

Inspiration 52: Now What?

Congratulations! You've journeyed through a year of inspiration, growth, and transformation. The 51 inspirations you've encountered have hopefully positively impacted you and your team, fostering a shift in mindset, nurturing growth, and offering a fresh perspective.

So, what's next? The journey doesn't end here. It's time to consolidate what we have learned and create a manifesto as a team. This manifesto should be simple yet capture the essence of this entire book. It's a compass that will guide us as we continue our journey towards high performance and team success.

Here's one of the manifestos I have previously created that I'm particularly proud of:

" In our quest for excellence and sustained high performance, we commit to dedicating time:

- I have dedicated discretionary time to improve myself.
- We have dedicated time to understand our client.

179

- We have dedicated time to build relationships.
- We have dedicated time to understand the system.
- We have dedicated time as a team to improve the system."

Interestingly, this last inspiration brings us back to where we started - sharpening the axe. As we close this book, remember that the journey of learning and growth is never-ending. Let's carry forward the spirit of these inspirations and continue to sharpen our axes.

I would like to leave you with a quote attributed to the great 13th-century Persian poet and moral philosopher Saadi of Shiraz:

> "The true traveller is not the one who intermittently speeds up and then becomes weary, but the one who persistently and continuously progresses."

WHAT YOU LEARNED:

1. Dedicate time to Continuous improvement
2. Develop MVPs iteratively
3. Resourcefulness: Getting the job done mindset instead of doing my job
4. Using empowering phrases as a leader
5. Fostering an environment of innovation
6. How to control your response in emotionally stressful situations
7. What is agile
8. How to deliver your features incrementally
9. Empowering teams to make decisions
10. What is scrum
11. The roles in scrum
12. Lean and focussing on flow instead of utilisation
13. Agile project management: Fixing time and cost and leaving scope variable
14. What is the Kanban method
15. Value stream mapping and continuous improvement
16. Systems thinking
17. Understanding the problem before jumping to solution mode

18. How metrics drive behaviours
19. Analysis vs synthesis and how to see the bigger picture
20. Understanding the unforeseen consequences of our decisions
21. Emotional intelligence
22. Empathy
23. Maintaining peak performance even when under stress
24. How to manage risk
25. Tips for effective remote meetings
26. Organisational designs impact on enterprise Architecture
27. Developing inspirational vision statements
28. The laws of agile
29. Servant leadership
30. How to influence
31. How to be a great coach
32. Resistance to change
33. Listening to understand
34. Diversity of thought in effective decision-making
35. Empiricism and validating our hypotheses
36. Playfulness as a defensive response to stressful situations
37. Types of bosses
38. How to develop organisations that thrive in uncertainty
39. Gemba and go see
40. Using cybernetics to create organisations that are resilient and successful
41. How to foster creativity in your teams
42. Asking powerful questions
43. Reducing the complexity of solutions

44. Moving from functional specialisation to cross-functional teams
45. Data-informed decision making
46. Using intuition to make better decisions in business
47. Why transformation programs fail
48. When waterfall is better than agile
49. How to be a more flexible and adaptable person
50. Constructing bulletproof arguments
51. Agile myths and facts
52. Creating a team manifesto

NOTES AND REFERENCES

1. Coles, Nicholas A., Larsen, Jeff T., and Heather C. Lench. "A meta-analysis of the facial feedback literature: Effects of facial feedback on emotional experience are small and variable." Psychological Bulletin (2019) 145(6): 610-651.
2. "System Archetypes and Emergent Futures: Reflections on Facilitating System Change," YouTube video, 1:00:26 , "FHI 360," April 24, 2024, www.youtube.com/watch?v=OqMAi4h9zVQ
3. The reality of the brain is a lot more complex than this, but the amygdala hijack remains a great metaphor to simplify, understand, and learn to remain in control in stressful situations.
4. Mazdak Abtin (Senior Agile Coach), in discussion with the author, Melbourne, Australia, November 2019.
5. L. David Marquet, *Turn the Ship Around!: A True Story of Turning Followers into Leaders*, (London: Portfolio/Penguin, 2013).
6. "Active CEO Podcast #151 Arash Arabi Defeat the Enemy Within." NRG2perform. March 19, 2021. Audio, https://nrg2perform.com/active-ceo-podcast-151-arash-arabi-defeat-the-enemy-within

7. "The Efficiency Paradox | Niklas Modig | TEDxUmeå," YouTube video, "TEDx Talks," April 24, 2024, www.youtube.com/watch?v=hGJpez7rvc0

8. "Kanban is not for the faint-hearted | Andrew Rusling and Arash Arabi," YouTube video, "ZoomOut by Sprint Agile," April 24, 2024, www.youtube.com/watch?v=W0uFeW-BLd7o

9. "From Agile Hell to the Prager's Law - Dr Daniel Prager & Arash Arabi on Theory of Constraints," YouTube video, "ZoomOut by Sprint Agile," April 24, 2024, www.youtube.com/watch?v=TXk0GxaHyK0

10. Peter M. Senge, *The Fifth Discipline: The Art and Practice of the Learning Organization* (New York: Doubleday/Currency, 1990).

11. O'Shaughnessy, Patrick T. "Parachuting Cats and Crushed Eggs the Controversy over the Use of DDT to Control Malaria." *Am J Public Health* 98, no. 11 (2008). https://www.ncbi.nlm.nih.gov/pmc/articles/PMC2636426/

12. Ibid.

13. Daniel Goleman et al., Building Blocks of Emotional Intelligence: 12 Leadership Competency Primers (Florence, MA: More Than Sound, 2017)

14. Conway's Law." Think Insights. Accessed April 24, 2024. https://thinkinsights.net/strategy/conways-law/

15. Denning, Steve. "Explaining Agile." Forbes, September 8, 2016. Accessed April 24, 2024. https://www.forbes.com/sites/stevedenning/2016/09/08/explaining-agile/

16. "Leadership Defined | Dave Ramsey," YouTube video, 7:10, "EntreLeadership," April 24, 2024, www.youtube.com/watch?v=JIRgSFQ45I8.

17. "Simon Sinek: Why Leaders Eat Last," YouTube video, "99U," April 24, 2024, www.youtube.com/watch?v=ReRcHdeUG9Y

18. Arash Arabi, *The Wise Enterprise: Reshape your organisation for the age of uncertainty* (Australia: Sprint Agile, 2020).

19. "151 - Make your business a "Wise Enterprise" | Ft. Arash Arabi," Podcast, "Team Guru Podcast," April 24, 2024, https://soundcloud.com/teamguru/151-make-your-business-a-wise-enterprise-ft-arash-arabi

20. "Using neuroscience & cybernetics to transform social organisations | Bobby Azarian & Arash Arabi," YouTube video, "ZoomOut by Sprint Agile," April 24, 2024, www.youtube.com/watch?v=umwlbNULf-w

21. Robert C. Martin, *Clean Code: A Handbook of Agile Software Craftsmanship* (NJ: Prentice Hall, 2009).

22. "Daniel Goleman on using both thought and feelings in decision making," YouTube video, "LeadersIn," April 24, 2024, www.youtube.com/watch?v=eOQjVCJYyas

23. Wikipedia Contributors. 'Iowa Gambling Task.' Wikipedia, last modified January 1, 2024. Accessed April 24, 2024. https://en.wikipedia.org/wiki/Iowa_gambling_task

24. "Losing from day one: Why even successful transformations fall short." McKinsey & Company. Accessed April 24, 2024. https://www.mckinsey.com/capabilities/people-and-organizational-performance/our-insights/successful-transformations

25. "EI Evolution Summit: Why Transformation Programs Fail." LinkedIn Live. Accessed April 24, 2024. https://www.linkedin.com/video/live/urn:li:ugc-Post:6828648094276571136/

26. Amdurer, Emily, Boyatzis, Richard E., Saatcioglu, Argun, Smith, Melvin L., Taylor, Scott N. "Long term impact of emotional, social and cognitive intelligence competencies and GMAT on career and life satisfaction and career success." Frontiers in Psychology 5 (2014). https://doi.org/10.3389/fpsyg.2014.01447

27. Daniel Goleman, Richard Boyatzis, Richard J Davidson, Vanessa Druskat, George Kohlrieser, *Adaptability: A Primer (The Building Blocks of Emotional Intelligence Book 3)* (Florence: More Than Sound, 2017).

FIN.

www.ingramcontent.com/pod-product-compliance
Lightning Source LLC
Chambersburg PA
CBHW040853210326
41597CB00029B/4824